The Problem of
A Consideration of Preser
Methods for M

Gilbert Murray

Alpha Editions

This edition published in 2024

ISBN 9789362511607

Design and Setting By
Alpha Editions
www.alphaedis.com
Email - info@alphaedis.com

As per information held with us this book is in Public Domain.
This book is a reproduction of an important historical work.
Alpha Editions uses the best technology to reproduce historical work
in the same manner it was first published to preserve its original nature.
Any marks or number seen are left intentionally to preserve.

Contents

PREFACE	- 1 -
CHAPTER I GERMANY AND FRANCE I. THE PREDICAMENT OF GERMANY	- 10 -
II. THE POSITION OF FRANCE	- 22 -
III. THE SOLUTION	- 26 -
CHAPTER II THE EAST	- 32 -
I. SYRIA, MESOPOTAMIA, EGYPT, AND INDIA	- 33 -
II. AN EASTERN POLICY	- 38 -
CHAPTER III RUSSIA AND ITS BORDERS	- 42 -
I. THE CIVIL WAR	- 43 -
II. RUSSIA'S NEIGHBOURS	- 46 -
CHAPTER IV PRE-WAR AND POST-WAR CAUSES OF STRIFE	- 49 -
I. ARMAMENTS	- 50 -
II. MARKETS AND FOOD	- 53 -
CHAPTER V THE LEAGUE OF NATIONS	- 56 -
FOOTNOTES	- 60 -

PREFACE

The publication of this little book was interrupted by an incident which made me realize how easy it is for one who spends much time in trying to study sincerely a political problem to find himself out of touch with average opinion. The discovery has made me re-read what I have written. But re-reading has not led to any weakening of my expressions, rather the reverse. I wish only to make a brief general statement about the point of view from which I write.

I start from the profound conviction that what the world needs is peace. There has been too much war, and too much of many things that naturally go with war; too much force and fraud, too much intrigue and lying, too much impatience, violence, avarice, unreasonableness, and lack of principle. Before the war I was a Liberal, and I believe now that nothing but the sincere practice of Liberal principles will save European society from imminent revolution and collapse. But I am conscious of a certain change of emphasis in my feeling. Before the war I was eager for large and sweeping reforms, I was intolerant of Conservatism and I laughed at risks. The social order had then such a margin of strength that risks could safely be taken. Now I feel a need above all things of the qualities that will preserve civilization. For that preservation, of course, Liberality in the full sense is necessary, and constant progress and a great development of democracy.

But what is needed most is a return to a standard of public conduct which was practised, or at least recognized, by the best Governments of the world before the war, and which now seems to have been shaken, if not shattered. I am not demanding in any wild idealist spirit that Governments should act according to the Sermon on the Mount—though they well might study it a good deal more than they do. I am only saying that they must get back to the standard of veracity, of consistency, of honesty and economy, and of intellectual competence, that we had from Peel or Lord Salisbury or Gladstone.

I do not say that is enough. It is emphatically not enough. We need in foreign policy and home policy a higher standard than we had before, the standard implied by the League of Nations in international affairs and the ideal of Coöperation in domestic affairs. But the first thing is to recover our wholesome tradition.

I think few serious students of public affairs will dispute that the long strain of the war, confusing our ideas of good and evil, and at times centring our hopes upon things which a normal civilized man regards with loathing, has resulted in a widespread degradation of political conduct. Things are done now, in time of peace, which would have been inconceivable before 1914. And they are done now because we grew accustomed to worse things during the war. I do not wish to attack any individuals; but, as an instance of what I mean, one finds a Ministerial newspaper complacently remarking that certain country towns sacked by the police in Ireland were very small and poor places in any case, and the sacking not nearly so complete as the sacking of Belgian towns by the Germans on less provocation. I find to-day (November 4, 1920) the Chief Secretary for Ireland announcing in the House of Commons that he has had a court of inquiry into the alleged murder of John Conway by the police, and presenting an official report that Conway "died from natural causes"; while at the same time the *Times* special correspondent writes: "I went to the cottage in Rock Street of John Conway, who was shot on Monday evening, and saw him lying on his bed with a bullet wound in the temple." This is one case out of dozens. It is not a slip or an isolated crime. I put it to any man who can remember the years before the war that this represents a startling degradation of the standard of government. Such things used to happen in Mexico; now they happen in Great Britain.

Of course I supported the war. I believe it was necessary. I make no self-righteous claim to throw the guilt of it upon others, who did the fighting by which I and mine were saved. Let me therefore try to make clear why certain things shock me profoundly, while I supported others which can loosely be called "just as bad."

One of the worst things about war, as Thucydides has remarked, is that it takes away your freedom and puts you in a region of necessity. You may choose whether or not to fight; but, once fighting, your power of choice has gone.

Take the treaty with Italy in 1915. Italy demanded a certain price, if she was to come into the war on our side. Another party in Italy was negotiating with the Germans, to see what inducement could be offered for Italy to come in on the other side. (I make no complaint whatever of the conduct of these Italian statesmen; they naturally consulted the interests of their country.) The price was high, and involved the transference to Italy of territory to which, on principles of self-determination, she had little claim. But who could refuse the price? War "is a violent master and teaches by compulsion."

Take the blockade of Germany. It was a slow and somewhat cruel weapon to employ, falling most severely on the most innocent classes. But Germany was trying to blockade us, and only our superior strength and skill at sea caused her plan to fail. It was part of the normal means of war, and of course we used it.

Then came an extension of it. Poland, most unhappy of European nations, was swept by alternate armies, conquered by the Germans, devastated and laid bare. The Poles were our allies. Our newspapers had accounts of the appalling distress in Poland—the roads strewn with skeletons, the almost complete blotting-out of children under seven, and the like. The Americans proposed to send food for the relief of the Poles. But we made objection. We did not allow food to go into Poland, to save our own allies, who were starving. Why? Because the Germans were still taking from the miserable country all the food they could wring out of it. And if the Americans brought in more food, undoubtedly the enemy would take more. There was no choice. We had to refuse the entry of the food ships. But the man who had to sign that order may well have wished he had died before the need came to him.

These results and necessities of war, though I have chosen none of a sensational kind, are very horrible. It is not easy to think of actions much more horrible. But they are not exactly crimes, they are not marks of degradation in those who order them, because they are done under the compulsion of war. The alternative in each case is something equivalent to helping the enemy.

At the end of the war, after the signing of an armistice on the basis of the Fourteen Points, there came at last a moment of free choice. It came after five years of unspeakable waste—five years during which the nations of Europe had become habituated to cruelty and "all pity choked with custom of fell deeds." I am anxious to avoid the faintest semblance of heat or exaggeration, but I think it can hardly be disputed that practically every economist agreed that Europe was on the brink of economic ruin and could only be saved by a quick revival of trade; every man of conscience, irrespective of political party, knew that the first condition for the recovery of civilization was a change from the war mind to the peace mind. Such a change could not happen in a night. It must needs be gradual. It could only be brought about by a strong and persistent lead from those who possessed the ear of the world and the confidence of their own people. Never in the whole course of modern history has there been a more magnificent opportunity than then lay before the British Prime Minister, never has there been a clearer call of plain duty. He was free, as men in public life are seldom free. Great Britain hung on his lips, and Europe was waiting for the lead of Great Britain. It was for him to choose plain good or plain evil. And he chose, deliberately, evil. He dissolved Parliament and appealed to the country in a General Election on a programme of frantic war passion, coupled with promises which he knew to be false, and which were ridiculed by every educated man among his surroundings. This man had before him a task and an opportunity so glorious that one can scarcely speak of it except in the language of religion. Many ordinary men would willingly give their lives if they could save their fellow creatures from sufferings and perils far less terrible than those which then threatened. And he could have saved them without any sacrifice. It needed only a little courage. For a week or ten days he hesitated. Then on December 11 he proclaimed his programme: the Kaiser's head; the punishment of enemy war-criminals; Germany to pay the whole cost of the war; Britain for the British; rehabilitation of those whom the war had broken.

At the time when this programme was put forward I felt bewildered. I did not realize that any one could be, I will not say so wicked, but so curiously destitute of generous ambition, so incapable of thinking greatly. And when I tried to find out what motive could lie at the back of a failure so incredible, I was told by his supporters that the Prime Minister was not thinking about the matters of which I was thinking. He was trying to get a very large majority in the House of Commons and to crush his old colleagues, and conceivable rivals, entirely out of existence. Of course he succeeded.

I hope I have put this statement forward without any malice or party feeling. The state of the world is far too serious to permit of either. And I hope that the profound and burning indignation which I undoubtedly feel has not biased my judgment. In any case, the conclusion that I wish to draw is not a personal but a general one. I doubt if such action would have been possible before the war in any constitutional statesman, not to speak of a clever and humane man like Mr. George. I doubt if the public opinion of any nation would have endured it. A nation in which such conduct is tolerated, and even approved, ought surely to pause and bethink itself. For it is not a particular reckless or unfortunate act which is thus condoned; it is a way of behaviour. It is a way of behaviour which has its origin in the methods of war, and of which the characteristic is that it gives the unscrupulous man the advantage over the scrupulous man, the cheat over the honest player, the violent and the criminal over those who obey the law. It fosters exactly those things which it is the business of civilized society to prevent. There are always lawless and dishonest men in every large community, as there are criminals in every army. There are always men who make profit out of their neighbours' extremity, who use advertisement to stifle truth, who jeer at all that is higher than themselves. But in a good social order they are not influential. They acquire power only in a society which, in external conduct, is losing its traditional standards and inwardly, in the words of Tolstoy's great condemnation, has forgotten God.

My criticism here is directed against my own country, and in particular against the British Prime Minister, not in the least because I have any anti-British bias. On the contrary, I think that in most of the international problems of Europe the influence of Great Britain, and in particular of the British Prime Minister, is generally an influence for good, though not nearly such a strong and clear influence as it might be. I confine these criticisms to our own policy because the scolding of foreign countries is a notoriously profitless task. The only criticism that has any chance of being useful is that of matters for which the critic or his readers have some degree of responsibility.

I believe profoundly in the traditions of Liberal England. As every one knows who has cared to read my writings, I look to the League of Nations as the main hope of the world, and to the British Commonwealth as the mainstay of the League of Nations. But, if it was ever doubtful, it is surely clear in the present state of the world that the Commonwealth cannot rest upon any secure foundation except the good-will of its members. And that good-will in its turn depends upon equal law, good government, and good faith.

It is not a new lesson that we have to learn: it is an old lesson that good Englishmen once knew better than any rulers the world has ever seen, though five years of madness have made it largely forgotten. But, as Lord Grey has said, the choice now before us is absolute; we must learn or perish.

It is in this belief and this spirit that I have written the following pages, which I hope, except to those who still live in some unsubstantial paradise of war-bred delusions, will cause no permanent offence, nor leave the impression that where I think others have made mistakes I imagine that I should make none.

Readers will see that I have aimed throughout at simplicity of outline. I have deliberately focused attention on the one central problem, how to avoid the causes of international strife. And out of the many and multifarious difficulties that confront our harassed Foreign Office to-day, I have concentrated on a few typical cases. I have omitted, for instance, any discussion of Turkey, Armenia, Persia, Ireland, and the relations between Great Britain and the United States. I have omitted Africa, where, unless the white man's methods of administration are reconsidered, one of the gravest of the world's future dangers may soon be in fermentation. And I have said nothing of the economic problem in Europe, especially in Austria. The International Financial Commission, summoned at Brussels by the League of Nations, has issued a report on this matter which no government can afford to neglect. Its first recommendations are disarmament and freedom of trade, but they will not be enough without some system of international credits by which production may be set going among those populations which at present have neither food nor raw materials nor the means of buying them.

Since an edition of this little book is asked for in America I feel constrained to add a few words to the Preface. It will be seen that I have said nothing about two subjects of the first importance, the Irish Question and the relations between Great Britain and the United States. The Irish Question is, under present conditions, a domestic matter, since Ireland forms by law part of the United Kingdom and has the right of full representation in the British Parliament. It only touches foreign policy through its effect on foreign opinion.

I do not therefore propose to discuss the Irish Question here. Personally I believe that a favourable prospect of settlement is to be found in the policy advocated by Mr. Asquith and Lord Grey, and loosely called "Dominion Home Rule." This would put Ireland roughly in the same position as the self-governing British colonies, and would at once have two very important effects. It would put an end to the present oppressions and would give Ireland the right to a seat at the Assembly of the League of Nations. But I fear that no settlement whatever is possible in Ireland until the present Government is replaced by some other with more sincerity in its purpose and less blood upon its hands. The accounts of British misdeeds which I read in the Sinn Fein Bulletin and in some American newspapers appear to me to be both exaggerated and one-sided. Men exasperated by persecution are not as a rule capable of giving a perfectly fair and benevolent account of the behaviour of their persecutors. But in spite of the Government's policy of rigorous concealment, the Irish can now appeal to the evidence of a witness as nearly unimpeachable as can be expected in human affairs, a County Court Judge appointed originally by the British Government itself. Judge Bodkin, in a report submitted to the British Government on cases of crime which came before his Court in Clare County at the Hilary Sessions of 1920, states: "There were in all 139 cases in which it was proved that the criminal injuries were committed by armed forces of the Government, and only in the five cases already mentioned were any witnesses examined to justify, deny, or explain. In no case was there any evidence to suggest that the victims had been guilty of any offence."

In answer to a report like this the Government allows no public inquiry, inflicts, so far as is known, no punishment on the criminals, awards no compensation to the victims, and yet does not take any legal steps against its accuser. Such conduct does not seem compatible with innocence.

Indeed the complicity of the Government, particularly of Mr. Lloyd George and Sir Hamar Greenwood, in the system of illegal outrages called "reprisals" is no longer disputed, and has especially been brought out in Parliament by a conservative member, Mr. Oswald Moseley. The exact degree of complicity is, of course, open to doubt. If I may give my own opinion for what it is worth, I suspect that at some time when the Irish police forces were disposed to resign or to strike owing to the constant danger of assassination in which the Government's policy required them to live, the Government gave their officers some assurance that, if they would only stay on, their own conduct in dealing with Sinn Feiners would not be too closely scrutinized. That was the usual method pursued by the Czar's Government when arranging pogroms.

The defence of the British Ministers is that they were faced from the outset by a very difficult situation, owing to the irreconcilable differences between the northeast corner of Ulster and the rest of Ireland. Anxious for Tory support they gave pledges, the exact tenor of which has not been divulged, to Sir Edward Carson, the Ulster leader, and thus tied their own hands. The condition of Ireland became increasingly embittered, till, shortly after Sir Hamar Greenwood's appointment, the extreme Sinn Fein party, refusing parliamentary action and unable to meet the English in battle, adopted a policy of assassination. The Government, much embarrassed, did just what most bad governments generally have done in other parts of the world. They tried to stamp out the Sinn Fein terror by organizing a terror of their own, meeting crime by still more formidable crime, and recklessly confusing the innocent with the guilty. At last they have succeeded in uniting all Catholic Ireland in such detestation of the British name that an Irishman will now never betray another Irishman, however guilty, to the British police, nor even feel that the killing of an Englishman is quite the same thing as murder. "Things being in this state," the Government pleads, "how can we be expected to govern Ireland according to civilized standards?" The answer is that they cannot, and had better make room for another Government which can.

I cannot tell how great an effect this Irish calamity has had in embittering the relations between America and Great Britain. I would only venture to lay before Americans of moderate views my conviction that the great mass of educated opinion in England joins with the Free Liberals and the Labour Party in utterly condemning the Government's Irish administration. This conclusion is derived from personal conversation with people of various parties, and from the overwhelming anti-Government votes in the bye-elections, and the increasing protests and rebellions among the Government's supporters in Parliament. I have to admit that this condemnation is not reflected in the House of Commons as a whole, an utterly abnormal House elected in a moment when not only the fever of war, but many other fevers and corruptions of the body politic were at their height. It is not even reflected adequately in the press. For the press in England, with a few most honourable exceptions, is in the hands of a small number of individuals who—to say the least of it—were not elected to their present position of power by the confidence of their countrymen nor appointed thereto on grounds of intellect or character or public spirit. England is admittedly not in a very healthy state of mind. But, even now, at her worst, she is a far better and more decent country than could be concluded from either the London press or the House of Commons.

The picture I have given of European affairs may, I can well see, be taken in either of two ways by an American. It may well confirm his determination to keep absolutely clear of a world at once so ill-directed and so miserable. The case for American isolation is very easy to state and to understand. What is there to attract America towards further coöperation with any of the larger European nations? France? I can imagine no sane statesmen wishing to be drawn into the orbit of France in her present mood or with her present prospects. Germany? The existing German Government seems good, but old enmities do not so quickly die down, and Germany has still to prove that she is an honest and a peaceful power. Russia? To ask the question is to answer it. England? Who would wish to coöperate with the British Government in holding down Ireland by "competition in crime," in reëstablishing her slippery grasp on Mesopotamia, laboriously pacifying India and Egypt, and struggling indefinitely against Russian conspiracies to destroy her influence in the Moslem world? How can an American wish to remit England's debt to America when she is at this moment invading Germany in order to collect "to the last farthing" a claim which the American delegates at the Peace Conference rejected as extortionate? And who would wish to increase the wealth of a Government which, immediately after the War to end War, is lavishing all it can afford, and more, on armaments and military expeditions? Other less plausible arguments could easily be added. The suggestion, for instance, that this country, or any party or any fraction of a party in this country, intends or ever intended to use the Japanese Alliance for a war against the United States is the merest moonshine, and has been repeatedly disproved by the terms of the old treaty and by the public statements of both parties. But, taking only arguments that have some basis of truth, the case for American isolation is very strong.

And yet it is the wrong case. It is based, I venture to think, first on a misunderstanding, and next on too narrow a point of view. A misunderstanding; because it is not coöperation in that sense which is asked of her. She is not asked to support the policies of any European nation.

The League of Nations is not an alliance. She is asked only to sit in council with the other nations—as free and unpledged as they, or, if she wishes, still more so—to help those who have suffered, and are in part still sick in body and brain with their suffering, to face the vast problems which now confront mankind, and which the rest of us have pledged ourselves to face in the spirit of peace and justice and common sense which we thought was characteristically American. It is based on too narrow a view, because all summary judgments of foreign nations are that, whether they end in praise or blame. "La noble, l'incomparable Angleterre" of M. Briand is just as remote from fact as the "brutal and bloody Britain" of Mr. Hearst. Nations are made up of masses of individuals, who differ among themselves within each nation just about as much as the citizens of one nation differ from those of another. In every nation there are numbers of criminals and numbers of fine men. In every nation's past there are black places and white. Only it so happens that just now, after a time of hideous suffering and wrong-doing, in the midst of a time of savage resentments and passions and great material difficulties, the nations of the world are from the depth of their hearts longing for some way of avoiding war and treating one another in future a little more openly and fairly than they have in the past. They know they must have disputes, and that when the disputes come it is one of two things; they must either talk them out or fight them out. They are meeting to talk them out. But how can the talk be quite frank and free, or how can the promises of peace and fair dealing carry full conviction, while the greatest and the least wounded of all the nations refuses to join in them, but sits aloof in silence, from time to time sharpening her sword?

G. M.

CHAPTER I
GERMANY AND FRANCE
I. The Predicament of Germany

A friend of mine was recently travelling in Germany in a third-class railway carriage. The engine was slow and in lack of oil. The carriages, once so clean, warm, and well lighted, were unlit, dirty, and bitterly cold. There was an air of broken nerves and misery among the passengers, and one woman was still sobbing from some indignity offered to her by a foreign official in the occupied area. Presently an old gentleman, apparently a lawyer of some eminence, broke out: "A reckoning must come. My little grandchildren are drinking in revenge with their mother's milk. In thirty years or thereabouts we shall settle accounts with France, and then we shall make"—he swept the air with his hand—"*tabula rasa!*"

"Herr Justizrat," answered a younger man, "did you take part in the war? I think not—you would be over the age. I was in the war for four years. . . . I agree with you that, in all probability, in thirty or forty years we shall settle our account with France and make *tabula rasa*. And in thirty or forty years after that France will have her reckoning with us and make *tabula rasa* of Germany; and then we again, and so on. But, if you will excuse me, Herr Justizrat, I do not find in the prospect any of the satisfaction which it appears to give you."

An incident of this sort may be significant or may not. It may be typical or may be exceptional. But my friend's experience seems exactly to agree with the report made by Herr Simons to the Reichstag in the last week of August, 1920, upon the attitude of the German Government towards the war then proceeding between Poland and Russia. The Entente Powers had invited Germany to take certain unneutral steps on the side of Poland; the Government had, as a matter of course, refused. The Soviet Government had also invited Germany to join in the war on their side, holding out the hope that such action by Germany would precipitate a Bolshevik revolution in Poland and other parts of eastern Europe and lead to an alliance capable of defying the Entente. The German Government, said Herr Simons, carefully considered these proposals, as it felt bound to consider any possible prospect of escape for Germany from the intolerable servitude imposed upon her by the Peace of Versailles, but decided that it was not in the public interest to accept them.

Thus the German Foreign Minister, a man respected by all parties, expresses in sober and thoughtful language much the same sentiment as the Justizrat in his passion. The Peace of Versailles has, like most settlements imposed by conquerors upon their beaten enemies, produced a condition so intolerable that the vanquished must be expected to seize the first favourable opportunity for fighting to free themselves. It has sown the seeds of future war.

Now, it was the great hope of English Liberals and those who agreed with them, that, contrary to almost all precedent, this war might be ended by a peace so high-minded and statesmanlike and far-seeing, so scrupulously fair to the vanquished and so single-mindedly set upon the healing of national wounds and the reconstruction of a shattered society, that the ordinary motives for a war of revenge would not exist, and the nations might really coöperate with one another to save all Europe from a common ruin. In 1914 and 1915, when war still seemed to Englishmen an almost incredible horror, and it was still necessary to appeal to men's consciences if we wished them to fight, volunteers were invited for a "war to end war." The statesmen who, in those days, were still the leaders of the country, were emphatic in stating that we were not engaged in any attempt to destroy or oppress the German people, but only "the military domination of Prussia." Even later, when the Liberal and idealist elements in the country withered in the poisonous air or were supplanted by more robust forces, it seemed as if President Wilson was upholding, with even greater insistence and emphasis, the banner of ultimate reconciliation as the goal of the war. For the war itself he prescribed "Force, Force to the utmost, Force without stint or limit, righteous and triumphant Force, which shall make Right the Law of the World and cast every selfish dominion down in the dust" (April 6, 1918); but, as soon as the Hohenzollerns were overthrown, he was for what he called "peace without victory," a peace with no element of revenge, "a new international order based upon broad and universal principles of right and justice" (February 11, 1918). Especial emphasis was laid on our good-will towards the German people. "We have no quarrel with the German people. We have no feeling towards them but one of sympathy and friendship" (April 2, 1917). "They did not originate or desire this hideous war . . . we are fighting their cause, as they will some day see it, as well as our own" (Flag Day, 1917).

It is not clear that this ideal was an impossible one. The war of Prussia against Austria in 1866 was unscrupulous and aggressive in its origin; but Bismarck meant it to end in a reconciliation after victory, and so it did. He secured a peace which left no sting of injustice behind it, Lincoln did not live to make the settlement with the South after the American Civil War; but enough is known of his intentions to make us sure that he intended to carry through at all costs a peace of reconciliation, extremely different from that which took place when he was gone. The British war against the Boers in 1899-1902, though open to the severest criticism in its origin, ended in a genuine peace of reconciliation in the settlement of 1906, for which the reward came rapidly and in full measure at the outbreak of the Great War. Had things been a little different in 1918, had President Wilson had the same support from his own people that he had from the best elements in Europe, had a Liberal or Labour Government been in power to make a settlement of the Great War like the settlement which followed the Boer War, had the popular influences of the time been better guided, Europe might have had a genuinely Liberal peace. Indeed, it seemed at the last moment almost certain that a Liberal peace had been secured. In an address to Congress on January 8, 1918, President Wilson laid down his memorable Fourteen Points to be observed in any treaty of peace with Germany. The first five may be especially noted:

1. Open covenants of peace openly arrived at, after which there shall be no private international understandings of any kind, but diplomacy shall always proceed frankly and in the public view.

2. Absolute freedom of navigation upon the seas outside territorial waters, alike in peace and in war, except as the seas may be closed in whole or in part by international action for the enforcement of international covenants.

3. The removal as far as possible of all economic barriers, and the establishment of an equality of trade conditions among all nations consenting to the peace and associating themselves for its maintenance.

4. Adequate guarantees given and taken that national armaments will be reduced to the lowest point consistent with domestic safety.

5. A free, open-minded and absolutely impartial adjustment of all colonial claims, based upon a strict observance of the principle that in determining all such questions of sovereignty the interests of the populations concerned must have equal weight with the equitable claims of the Government whose title is to be determined.[1]

The Fourteen Points were not only acclaimed by Liberal opinion in England: they were vigorously circulated by our Government propaganda in Germany and Austria, as were all other statements considered likely to induce the enemy peoples to weaken or surrender. On October 5, 1918, the German Republican Government proposed peace on the basis of the Fourteen Points. "They requested President Wilson to take into his hands the task of establishing peace on the basis of the Fourteen Points contained in his message to Congress of January 8, 1918, and on the basis of his subsequent proclamations, especially his speech of September 27, 1918."

Later on they asked the President to inquire if the Allied Governments also agreed to them. In response to his inquiries the Allied Governments sent in to him an identical memorandum:

The Allied Governments have given careful consideration to the correspondence which has passed between the President of the United States and the German Government. Subject to the qualifications which follow, they declare their willingness to make peace with the Government of Germany on the terms of peace laid down in the President's address to Congress of January 8, 1918, and the principles of settlement enunciated in his subsequent addresses. They must point out, however, that what is usually described as the Freedom of the Seas is open to various interpretations, some of which they could not accept. They must therefore reserve to themselves complete freedom on this subject when they enter the Peace Conference.

One further "qualification" was made by the Allied Powers: by the "restoration" of the invaded territories they understood "that compensation would be made by Germany for all damage done to the civilian population of the Allies and their property by the aggression of Germany by land, by sea and from the air."

Thus the Fourteen Points were converted into a solemn international agreement. The Allies agreed that the treaty of peace should consist of the application in detail of that fundamental document. On that understanding the Germans laid down their arms and surrendered their means of defence.

It is always difficult in the affairs of a democratic country to determine the exact point where mere inconsistency and laxity of thought, or even mere lack of coördination between the various organs of government, merge into something like deliberate perfidy. It may so easily happen that one set of individuals give the promise and quite another set act in breach of it. But an Englishman who wishes seriously to understand the present international situation must begin by realizing clearly that the treaty imposed on the Germans at Versailles, after they had surrendered their arms, appears to them and to a large number of neutral observers as a monstrous breach of faith. It contravened in spirit and in detail much of what they understood by the Fourteen Points. I confess that, after reading carefully the German Protest and the Allied Reply, it seems to me that the German reading of President Wilson's terms was in some points the natural one; and, apart from the treaty itself, that the action taken against the Germans when they were disarmed was not consistent with the language and the pledges addressed to them while they were still in the field. As a matter of fact, certain of those responsible, or partly responsible, for the negotiations on the Entente side, when they saw the way things were going, recalled bitterly the great historic perfidy by which Rome trapped Carthage to her doom.

A charge of this kind is, of course, very serious; and the results of the action taken at Versailles have been more than serious. I will ask my readers patiently to consider in broad outlines the causes, psychological and other, which seem to have been at work; for of course it is quite possible and even probable that, of the main actors concerned, not one had any intention of trying to trap the Germans by perjury. Some of them doubtless were unscrupulous men, such as wars habitually throw to the surface; but they were not men of the Machiavellian type.

Two broad facts stand out clearly to one who studies the documents. First, the Governments which accepted President Wilson's Fourteen Points as the basis of peace with Germany were from the start quite out of sympathy with his spirit. Why, then, did they accept them? Because they had really no choice. To refuse would not have been only to reject a long delayed and desperately needed peace. It would have been to confess to the world that, contrary to so many previous professions, their aims were frankly what is now termed "imperialistic." Above all, it would have been to alienate Mr. Wilson, without whom victory was impossible. They were bound to accept.

But Mr. Wilson's language was often rather lacking in definiteness. Who knows exactly what "justice" is, or what may be regarded as consideration for "the true interests" of the German people? They accepted the terms; but they were free to use all permissible ingenuity in interpreting a document which they had not drawn up, and which had been forced upon them in a time of need.

Furthermore, one who labours through the four hundred and forty articles of the treaty, with their innumerable subdivisions, will find not merely that the treaty represents broadly the victory of the right side over the wrong, and is a charter of emancipation to large parts of Europe. He will find also that four hundred or more of the detailed articles are reasonable enough and many of them excellent. The injustice arises in two ways. First, that on every doubtful point, and there are many, the decision is apt to be given against the enemy; and next, that behind the respectable structure of the treaty there existed in fact a flood of white-hot war-passion—revenge, hate, terror, suspicion, and raging covetousness—which poisoned the atmosphere and here and there made a breach in the protecting wall.

A great English military critic somewhat shocked public opinion by saying at the time of the armistice, "This armistice is wrong. We have got them down, and now we ought to kick them till we have had enough." The French, he said, ought to have continued the war and marched on to Berlin, plundering and ravaging till they had satisfied their revenge. The words sound like insanity, but the speaker explained them later on. A war of revenge, he argued, is within the limits of pardonable human nature. And it comes to an end. But, being cheated of their decisive campaign of victory, the French were making a peace of revenge; and that is a thing which is apt to admit of no forgiveness and no finish.

I quote these words not because I agree with them in practical policy, but because of the profound psychological truth that they express. Behind the statesmen who had pledged their words, however unwillingly, remained masses of ignorant, violent, and war-maddened people, many of them with terrible wrongs to avenge and no guide or leader to help them against themselves. We need not recall, though few sensitive people will ever forget, the horrors of the propaganda of hate. It is only worth realizing that the mob-inspired journalists and journalist-inspired mobs who clamoured for an utter and all-devouring peace of revenge, including the starvation and enslavement of half Europe for thirty or fifty or a hundred years, had never themselves signed the Fourteen Points and felt no personal inconsistency or turpitude if they compelled the Supreme Council of the Allies to break its faith.

The first step in this policy lay outside the treaty. The third of the Fourteen Points established "equality of trade conditions" and the "removal of economic barriers" between all the nations consenting to the peace. Immediately after the armistice a proposal was made, and met with strong American support, that the Allies should set themselves at once to attempting to cope with the threatened famine and the lack of raw materials in Central Europe, and thus get European trade on its legs again as early as possible. This would relieve a vast amount of distress, serve as a stepping-stone to reconciliation, save many nations from the danger of irremediable collapse, and also make far more possible the restoration of the invaded areas and the payment of large reparations by Germany. It was proposed to follow the analogy of the peace of 1871; to draw up a preliminary peace agreement, stating principles and limits but not details. For example, it might be agreed that Germany must surrender some territory in the West and in Poland, but not beyond certain geographical lines; must pay an indemnity to be fixed on certain principles, but not to exceed a certain sum, and the like. The territorial agreement, again, might be based on the elaborate statement of war aims issued by the British Government on January 10, 1917. The Germans could have accepted this, and the work of reconstruction been begun immediately. Incalculable distress and suffering would thus have been saved.

But another view prevailed. With the short-sightedness that so often accompanies brutality, the German High Command had, in the very last months of the war, when their defeat was certain, tried systematically to cripple the industry of Belgium and France by destroying mines, breaking machinery, carrying off movable plant, and the like. Their own manufacturing plant was undamaged, and they indulged in the fatuous expectation that they might recapture their lost markets and spring into prosperity, while France and Belgium were still too crippled to commence work. Of course, this could not be allowed. The obvious alternatives, such as allocating certain German factories to French or Belgian companies whose plant had been destroyed, or simply allocating the profits to purposes of reparation, appear not to have been considered. The blinder motives were too strong, and no statesman arose to give guidance. All Germany must be punished. She had not been invaded and ravaged. She must be made to suffer the pains of invasion. She must be ravaged in cold blood. The complete ruin of Germany, argued certain French journalists and politicians, was demanded by all considerations both of justice and of safety, and it had not by any means been attained. Russia was paralyzed and wrecked by Bolshevism. But the German Revolution had been carried successfully through. The people were not yet demoralized, and the problem was how to demoralize them. Perhaps starvation would do it. Hence was started the policy of deliberately ruining Germany, after her surrender, by a long blockade in time of what, to the ordinary man, appeared to be peace, and immediately after a promise of "the removal of economic barriers and the establishment of equality of trade conditions." This was not a technical breach of faith; technically we were still at war with Germany, and we had never promised not to starve our enemies after their surrender. The promise of equality of trade conditions only applied to conditions after the peace. Nevertheless, a historian will probably regard the establishment and continuance of this blockade of the enemy lands after their surrender as one of those many acts of almost incredible inhumanity which have made the recent Great War conspicuous in the annals of mankind and shaken thoughtful men's faith in the reality of modern civilization. Certain articles in the *Matin* discussing the exact dose of famine desirable in order to create the maximum of individual suffering and public weakness in the Boche are difficult to parallel in the literature of morbid hate, except among some of the German war pamphlets.

Thus the Fourteen Points, besides a regrettable indefiniteness of phrasing, had the fatal fault of being utterly out of touch with the feeling of most of the belligerents. As the time wore on this feeling asserted its influence on the terms of the treaty. The Boche had deliberately and treacherously plunged Europe into war; he had waged the war with revolting cruelty; he had inflicted unheard-of suffering on the innocent, and, by a miracle, he had been beaten. Now let him pay the penalty! President Wilson had pledged the Allies "to be just to the German people as to all others.... To propose anything but justice to Germany at any time would be to renounce our own cause." "Very good," answered the dominant voices of 1918; "the criminal asks for justice, and so far as our power reaches, justice he shall have!" The total of wrongs done by Germany, in plotting the war, in waging it, and in the destruction of life and property, could easily be regarded as an almost infinite sum, and "Justice" surely demanded for that an almost infinite punishment.

The first concession to this insistent pressure was on a point of form. The language of the Fourteen Points and the accompanying documents implied that the treaty would be a matter of discussion and negotiation. The basis was agreed upon; it seemed natural to suppose that the next step was to negotiate. But popular feeling had caught at the phrase "unconditional surrender"; and, though nothing could be clearer than the fact that the German army had surrendered on perfectly explicit conditions, signed and agreed to by every Government concerned, it was decided that terms were not to be negotiated but "imposed." Mr. Keynes has shown in an interesting way how great was the effect of this decision. Terms were drawn up with a view to bargaining, leaving a margin for possible concessions; and then there was no bargaining. The whole demand was suddenly enforced.

Questions of territory outside Europe were decided purely by conquest. Immense areas in Asia and Africa were seized as spoil by the strongest Powers, though the conditions of their tenure were, so it was hoped, to be regulated by the League of Nations. In some cases there was a pretence of consulting the wishes of the inhabitants; in most cases this was not practicable. In Syria and South Tyrol the wishes of the inhabitants were notoriously overridden. In Europe as a whole, however, the decisions were made on Wilsonian principles. True, they told heavily against Germany. But as a matter of fact the Germans and German Austrians, by reason of their great strength and high organizing power, had an imperial position in Europe, and any liberation of subject or quasi-subject nationalities was bound to be at the expense of the Germans. The territorial settlement, in spite of the great and needless distress produced by the break-up of the Austro-Hungarian system, is on principles of nationality juster than that which preceded it. The more extreme anti-German claims were successfully resisted. France was not allowed to annex Germany up to the Elbe, as M. Hanotaux wished; nor even up to the Rhine. No partition of Germany by force was permitted, though an agitation for that purpose still continues in France and the prohibition of any future union between German-Austria and the rest of Germany was actually embodied in the treaty. The treaty of Berlin had in just the same way attempted to forbid the unity of Bulgaria.

As regards the penal clauses, it may be convincingly argued that the great crimes and cruelties and breaches of law which have signalized this war ought emphatically to meet with judgment and punishment from some tribunal representing the conscience of civilized mankind. On grounds of justice the presence of such penal clauses in the treaty could be amply justified, though considerations of policy make it more questionable. But all thoughts of equal justice disappeared in derision when it was found that only crimes committed by the enemies of the Entente were to be punished; crimes committed by British, French, Italian, Serbian or American criminals were privileged acts, to which "Justice" had nothing to say.

This absurd clause has, of course, given rise to suspicions, more absurd than itself, of dark crimes committed by Entente generals which must be concealed at any cost. Such suggestions are nonsense. Indefensible as it is, the clause was dictated by no more sinister passion than ordinary national vanity. The economic clauses were open to graver suspicions. It was whispered that trade interests of not quite unimpeachable character had some influence with members of the French, the Italian, and even the English Government; and the old German accusation that England entered the war in order to destroy a trade rival, utterly untrue at the time, seemed to receive some colour by the terms of peace. Germany depended for her prosperity on her industry and her overseas trade. Her industry was wrecked by an immense demand upon her coal. The mines of Lorraine, the Saar Valley, and, subject to plebiscite, of Silesia, were handed over to other states; and out of the remainder Germany was condemned to pay an amount of coal which proved, on investigation at Spa, two years later, to be beyond her powers. Her overseas trade was annihilated at a blow by the seizure of all the vessels of her mercantile marine exceeding 1600 tons gross and a large proportion of her small vessels and fishing-boats, combined with a demand upon such ships as she might build in future. Her voice was stifled by the seizure of all her telegraphic cables: news henceforth was to be a monopoly of the conquerors. At the same time all her colonies were taken from her. She was forbidden to set up any tariffs for her own protection. Her navigable rivers were put under the control of international commissions on which the Germans or Austrians were a small minority. And while it was somewhat unctuously explained to Germany that in a virtuous world trade would be free and untrammelled, and that the commissions only intended to see that she did not erect barriers against her innocent neighbours, there was no provision whatever made to debar the Allies from erecting what barriers they pleased against Germany. "It would appear to be a fundamental fallacy," declared the Allied Reply, "that the political control of a country is essential in order to procure a reasonable share of its products. Such a proposal finds no foundation in economic law or history." It has found some foundation in history since.

The triumph of penal ingenuity, however, was the indefinite indemnity. It was agreed on both sides that Germany was to pay an indemnity. She did not demur. Indeed, her mouth was closed by the monstrously oppressive and inhuman proposals various Germans had themselves put forward when they expected to win the war. She had openly intended to "bleed France and England white." Now that she was beaten she was prepared to pay. She accepted the duty of "restoring" the invaded territories. This was defined as "reparation for all damage done to the civil population of the Allies by German aggression." The Germans probably understood this to mean the damage done to civilian life and property by invasions or raids; but they were told that this view was too narrow. Every soldier killed or wounded had civilians dependent on him; nay, he himself was really a civilian forced by German aggression to desert his business. All his business losses, the separation allowances to his wife, the pensions to ex-soldiers or to their dependents, all damage to any one's "health or honour," were ultimately "due to German aggression" and should be paid by Germany. No such terms had ever been heard of before, true; but the British electors had been promised that "Germany should pay the whole cost of the war"; and the sense of the solemn contract was distorted to suit the election cry. After 1871 the Germans had imposed on France what was then considered the extremely severe indemnity of two hundred million pounds sterling. Some experts now proposed two thousand million sterling as an adequate indemnity to be paid by Germany, others three thousand million. That was emended by popular orators to ten thousand million; thirty thousand million; fifty thousand million. Absurd to say that Germany could not pay! If all German property were confiscated and all Germans for seventy-five years were made to work for the Allies at a bare subsistence wage, a well-known English public man was prepared to get more than fifty thousand million out of them.

The Americans bluntly refused to endorse demands which they considered extortionate. The indemnity was left unspecified. It should depend on Germany's capacity to pay. Let the Germans get to work at once and do their best. The more they produced, the more the Allies would take; and if, after two years or so, it became necessary to fix the sum, the less the Germans had produced in those two years the less they would eventually have to pay. It is said that some of the British Ministers, secretly anxious to be more reasonable than was consistent with popularity at the moment, wished to postpone the fixing of the indemnity until the rage of their own "Khaki Election" should have cooled down. But their calculation was a bad one. As the German delegation observed: "The German people would feel themselves condemned in slavery, because everything they accomplished would benefit neither themselves nor even their children, but merely strangers. But the system of slave labour has never been successful."

For the purpose of raising money the proposal was merely fatuous. It took away from the Germans every possible motive for producing wealth. But its object in some minds was not money: its object was the permanent ruin of Germany. It was feared in France that, though the Germans were now exhausted and beggared, their notorious industry and ingenuity might in time enable them to pay off their indemnity and rise again to affluence and strength. So it was arranged that, for some years at least, they should be deprived of every motive for industry.

Lastly, a new provision was made about private property. The rule hitherto observed in the land wars of civilized states was that enemy private property was respected, and if seized during the war was restored at the conclusion of peace. This rule was, of course, enforced in favour of any property belonging to nationals of the Entente countries situated in enemy lands; but reciprocity was not admitted. The private property of any German situate in any part of the world which was under the control of the Ententes was *ipso facto* confiscated. "The Allied and Associated Powers reserve the right to retain and liquidate all" such property. Every German, however innocent, who had settled in our territory before the war was thus exposed to be robbed of everything he possessed. Nay, it seems almost incredible, but in the original form of the treaty which was put before the enemy for signature the stipulation seems actually to have been laid down that any property which a German might hereafter make or acquire in Entente territory should be liable to confiscation at the will of the Entente Governments! This clause was too much even for the atmosphere of Versailles, and in response to the German protest the stipulation about the future was dropped.[2] For the rest of the confiscation, the Entente Reply brazens it out with the remark that the property is not really taken from the individual, as his own Government can always pay him back! And in case the private property of Germans in neutral countries should have an unfair advantage, the Reparation Commission obtained special powers for confiscating that too, up to the limit of £100,000,000.

We need not stop to consider whether there was any extraordinary exhibition of "Teutonic insolence" in the action of certain German officials who resigned their offices rather than sign this treaty; nor need we swell the chorus of English, French, Italian, and American newspapers in expressing the natural horror of those refined nations at the bad manners of Count Brockdorf-Rantzau in actually breaking a paper-knife in the stress of his emotion, when, under protest, he consented to sign. There was one man among the British representatives who had known what it was to be conquered after a desperate war. General Smuts was a man of imagination as well as a soldier and a statesman. He hesitated long before signing the treaty; and when, in the end, he decided that it was necessary to do so, he immediately published a statement of protest. "I have signed the peace treaty, not because I consider it a satisfactory document, but because it is imperatively necessary to close the war.... The six months since the armistice was signed have perhaps been as upsetting, unsettling, and ruinous to Europe as the previous four years of war. I look upon the peace treaty as the close of those two chapters of war and armistice, and only on that ground do I sign it." Liberal opinion in England muttered assent. Some important officials resigned. But the fear of upsetting peace altogether prevented any open protest in Parliament. We need not lose ourselves in speculations as to the strange devices to which public men can sink when their self-interest is clear and their responsibility can be denied or evaded; nor yet as to the infinite ramifications by which war spreads its poison through human society, a thing twice-cursed, cursing him that strikes and him that suffers. The old German Government had committed a vast crime against humanity; its people had backed it up, as all European peoples back up their own Governments, and could not expect to escape heavy punishment. The one question we need ask ourselves is this: Is it not as certain, as anything in human nature can be, that a treaty of such a character, imposed on a conquered nation by force, if not also by treachery, will, as a matter of course and without the faintest scruple, be broken as soon as there is a favourable opportunity for breaking it? Of course the Germans will break it if they can; and of course they will make another war, call it a war of revenge or a war for freedom as you please, as soon as there is any chance of winning it.

So said the Justizrat in the train. So, in effect, says Herr Simons; so almost *ad nauseam* repeat all the German Conservative and patriotic newspapers. It is difficult to see how any German who is not a convinced pacifist should do otherwise than prepare with all his energies for the next war, unless some other way is made possible of escape from a tormenting servitude.

II. The Position of France

If that is so, what is the position of France? France in 1914 was forced into a war which she tried hard to avoid. The French suffered horribly and fought heroically. They sacrificed everything to the war. And we, who know what our own people paid in broken nerve, in bitterness, and in economic dislocation, cannot be surprised that France has paid a heavie price. They escaped defeat by the help of England, Russia, Italy, and America; without these powerful allies they would certainly have been defeated. We need not try to estimate exactly what their fate would have been if they had lost the late war, because if they lose the next their treatment will be infinitely worse. It will be, as far as possible, *tabula rasa*. It will be the passing of the horse-hoofs of Attila. Meantime France's allies are, naturally enough, going home and attending to their own businesses; her population is much smaller than Germany's and increases even more slowly.

A French statesman of the type of M. Poincaré or M. Hanotaux makes himself no illusions. Germany is the enemy. Germany will fight again as soon as she is strong enough. Therefore she must never be allowed to become strong enough. M. Hanotaux, who was Foreign Minister during the years 1894-98, when French foreign policy was more ably managed than now, has recently published a book in criticism of the Treaty of Versailles. He does not deal in any Wilsonian phrases about justice or humanity; he considers the treaty solely with a view to the security of France, and he finds it sadly wanting. And a large mass of opinion, probably the prevailing opinion, in France supports him.

First of all, it must be remembered, France wanted, and thought she had received, a special guarantee against future German attacks in the form of a defensive Alliance between France, England, and America. The representatives at Paris had agreed to this treaty, which definitely pledged England and America to come again to the help of France in case of another unprovoked attack by Germany. The English Parliament amid some protests, ratified the treaty, but the United States Senate threw it out, and therewith the treaty ceased to be binding on England.

I think, after considerable hesitation, that the rejection of the treaty was a misfortune. Formally, no doubt, it was open to objection. It seemed like an unnecessary excrescence upon the Covenant of the League of Nations, which already gave guarantees against war. It contravened one of Mr. Wilson's principles, and a very sound one, laid down on September 27, 1918: "Thirdly, there can be no leagues or alliances or special covenants and understandings within the general and common family of the League of Nations." Yet the practical importance of reassuring France was so urgent that a little formal incorrectness might have been worth incurring; and even formal incorrectness could have been avoided by the simple expedient of making this guarantee to France take the form of a special rider to Article XVI of the Covenant.

That article provides: "Should any member of the League resort to war in disregard of its covenants under Articles XII, XIII, or XV, it shall *ipso facto* be deemed to have committed an act of war against all other members of the League, which hereby undertake immediately to . . ." To do what? One expects that they will undertake to declare war, and this is what the French wanted. But no. They only undertake to apply an economic boycott to the offending state, while the Council may "recommend to the several Governments concerned what effective military, naval, or air force they shall severally contribute to the armed forces to be used to protect the covenants of the League." In case of a future attack by Germany on France, France's late allies are bound to boycott German trade, but are not explicitly bound to give military help to France. I suggest that it would have been possible for Great Britain and America to add a rider stating specifically that in one of the cases contemplated by this article, namely, an unprovoked attack on France by Germany, they would not merely proclaim a blockade and consider what to do next, but would immediately and unconditionally declare war. Such an undertaking would involve some risk and be contrary to our usual policy; but I am inclined to suggest that the risk would have been worth taking.

However, this was not done. France was left with the impression that if attacked she could not count with confidence on the military support of her late allies or of the other Powers of the League. The result was disastrous. While the rest of Europe, supported by a small but generous and brilliant band of French radicals and Socialists, considered the Treaty of Versailles intolerably harsh, the dominant French policy complained that it was inadequate for her protection. The line of criticism was somewhat as follows:

1. Germany should have been broken up. No peace should have been made with Germany as a whole, but separate treaties of peace with Saxony, Bavaria, Westphalia, Prussia, etc. These states should have been provided with separate systems of coinage, postage, tariffs, laws, etc., so as to make the diversity stable and permanent. They should be forbidden ever to unite. Also, France should have annexed a large part of Germany; not up to the Rhine—which was the view of Marshal Foch—but up to the Elbe. The occupation of this territory might impose a burden on France, but burdens

must be borne when such important purposes are involved. And after all the cost could be charged to the Germans! . . .

As this simple precaution was not taken, the next best thing is to keep Germany weak. Starve her by the blockade till sheer misery produces a Bolshevik revolution and society collapses in common ruin. Then apply the indefinite indemnity, not from the desire to get money, but to prevent Germany again raising her head.

2. Since France's late allies cannot be relied upon, she must make by diplomacy new allies whose hands she can force, and who occupy a convenient geographical situation. Poland is in just the right place. Let France help Poland and stimulate Polish ambitions. She too is a nation maddened by suffering and now dazzled by success. A great imperialist Poland, on bad terms with her neighbours, but backed by France, will need a large and effective army, and will be ready to strike at Germany's rear the moment she attempts to move westward. Unfortunately, Poland is apt to be on bad terms with Russia; and as things now are Russia is so much the enemy of the Entente that she is thrown into the arms of Germany. That is deplorable and must not be allowed to continue. The Bolsheviks must be overthrown and a Government set up in Russia which is dependent for its existence on French support. As an additional safeguard, perhaps it will be necessary to secure a pro-French Hungary, to back up the pro-French Poland. But we must not despair yet of overthrowing the Bolsheviks.

3. Lastly, France herself needs more soldiers. And she knows where to get them! The late King Leopold of Belgium once said to M. Hanotaux, "Qu'est-ce que vous cherchez en Afrique, vous autres Français?" and M. Hanotaux replied, "Sire, des soldats!" France during the war established conscription in her African territories and, in spite of a somewhat bloody rebellion by the ignorant savages, who thought the slave trade was being reëstablished, succeeded in importing to France a black army which at one time numbered 600,000 fighting men. With a little more energy and greatly increased territories, that number might be trebled. France is a smaller nation than Germany; but France plus Algeria, Tunis, Morocco, Senegambia, French Congo, and the new German territories is a much larger nation than Germany without colonies. And blacks fortunately have not the same rights as white men!

A permanently wrecked Germany, vast black armies for France, armed allies always ready on Germany's eastern frontier; with these conditions fulfilled, France, it is hoped by these politicians, may at last breathe freely.

What is wrong with this policy? You may call it devilish, if you will, since it is based on the deliberate and artificial creation of human misery; but is it bad policy? After all, air-bombs and poison gas and the like may be called devilish. But, devilish or not, they have sometimes to be used. If Germany is certainly and confessedly looking out for the next opportunity of escaping from the consequences of the treaty and retrieving her fortunes on the battlefield, is not France bound to take every precaution to see that Germany shall never be strong enough to do so with success? The next war will be far worse than the last. The terms imposed on the beaten party will be even more desolating and destructive. France is probably a less vigorous plant than her enemy. She has failed to kill Germany, but Germany might succeed in killing her.

It seems that Germany is absolutely bound to fight, if there is no other way of recovering her freedom and her right to live, while France is absolutely bound to hold her enemy down mercilessly, if there is no other way of securing her own safety.

III. The Solution

But perhaps after all there is. Last among the Fourteen Points came the proposal to found "A general Association of Nations under specific covenants for the purpose of affording mutual guarantees of political independence and territorial integrity to small and great states alike." The Treaty of Versailles has after all two faces. It had to express two great waves of feeling and two international necessities. Mr. Wilson was not so utterly "bamboozled" as Mr. Keynes would have us believe. General Smuts and Lord Robert Cecil were not so utterly without influence on the settlement. The least depressing paragraphs in the Allied Reply to the German delegation are those in which they explain that the terrific severity of the greater part of the treaty applies only to a "transition period" of punishment, of reparation and of trial, at the end of which they see the realization of Mr. Wilson's promises. "The conditions of peace contain some provisions for the future which may outlast the transition period during which the economic balance"—between Germany and the invaded countries—"is to be restored; and a reciprocity is foreseen after that period which is very clearly that equality of trade conditions for which President Wilson has stipulated." The phrasing of the paragraph is awkward, but the main drift is clear. The Fourteen Points are accepted, but adjourned; when Germany has been punished and reparation made, they will come into force. "The Allied and Associated Powers look forward to the time when the League of Nations established by this treaty shall extend its membership to all peoples." "They see no reason why Germany should not become a member of the League in the early future," provided she satisfies certain tests. "It has never been their intention that Germany or any other Power should be indefinitely excluded from the League of Nations." They are convinced that the Covenant of the League "introduces an element of progress into the relations of peoples which will develop and strengthen to the advantage of justice and of peace."

This is as it should be; but the world does not stand still while Germany is making reparation and being taught gradually to love her chastisers. If the League "introduces an element of progress," the sooner it gets to work the better. It is only too clear that every month which passes with the League entirely dominated by England, France, and Italy encourages and deepens the suspicion with which the League is regarded by its critics. I say nothing of American criticisms, in which many factors coöperate. But the Swiss Federal Council, in the very able and persuasive message which it issued to the Assembly on February 17, 1920, in favour of joining the League, has to deal with this suspicion. "One has been tempted at times to consider the League as an alliance of the conquerors against the conquered. The fact that Germany, Austria, and the former Russian Empire remain provisionally excluded from the League may have given a semblance of truth to this manner of thinking." The suspicion is afterwards described as "this apparently accurate criticism." Switzerland as a whole has fortunately rejected the suspicion and by a small majority joined the League. But in most of Central Europe the League of Nations movement is strangled in its birth by the general feeling that the present League means merely the Entente Powers and their clients, and the elements for starting a counter-league are consolidating month by month. This counter-league would probably not be an open and confessed alliance. But Russia, Germany, and the United States are still outside, and there are many unpaid grudges amongst the Moslems of Asia. The test which is exacted by Article I from any new state desiring to become a member of the League is that "it shall give effective guarantees of its sincere intention to observe its international obligations." Interpreted with theological strictness, this would probably result in the rejection of all candidates, to say nothing of the expulsion of many of the original members. Perfect sincerity in observing unpleasant obligations is not a common characteristic of human societies. But in the ordinary sense of the words the test is already satisfied by Germany and Austria and most of the succession states. The Assembly of the League meets for the first time on November 15, 1920. It ought not to dissolve without admitting to its membership Germany and Austria, as well as several other candidates who have already applied. At the moment of writing (November, 1920), Lord Grey, Lord Selborne, and Mr. Barnes have issued a joint appeal for the immediate admission of Germany, which has long been the accepted policy of the League of Nations Union. There are many obstacles, but the result will doubtless be known before these words are in print. Fortunately, the admission of new members is decided by a two-thirds majority of the Assembly and does not require a unanimous vote. Once the League is established on a broad base, including the conquered nations on equal terms with the victorious, the prospect of that war of revenge which has hitherto seemed almost inevitable will dwindle and become remote.

The hope expressed above has not been realized. Austria, Bulgaria, and many less important states applied for admission to the League and were accepted, but French feeling was known to be very strong, and Germany did not even apply. Had she done so she would probably have had a majority in her favour, and it was considered until the beginning of March, 1921, that she was certain of admission at the next meeting of the Assembly in September. But in the meantime untoward events have taken place.

The French Government, like the English, obtained success at the elections by wild promises to make Germany pay all the costs of the war. As M. Poincaré has observed, "the French people will not understand how the victors in a great war can be on the verge of bankruptcy." Consequently they think their rulers are cheating them. Educated people, in France as in England, have long since ceased to expect much from German indemnities, but the Governments still depend on their appeal to mob-psychology; and it was believed that if M. Briand ventured to make any concessions in the direction of reason or moderation he would lose his majority in the Chamber. The proposals made at the Inter-Allied Conference at Brussels and drawn up by the French expert, M. Seydoux, had been silently dropped as unsatisfying; the subsequent British proposals made at Boulogne had been rejected for the same reason. It was necessary, however, to make some definite proposals to Germany without much further delay, since the treaty had laid down May 1, 1921, as the time for a settlement. Germany was by that time to have paid a thousand million pounds on account, and was to learn the extent, finite or infinite, of the total bill. Mr. Lloyd George, as might have been expected, showed much sympathy with M. Briand in his awkward position, and agreed to a demand for reparations on a scale which was obviously fantastic. It began, reasonably enough, with a system of annuities, though the first figure was probably too high and the last figures can scarcely have been meant seriously. Germany was to pay £150,000,000 a year for the first five years; then the annual sum was to increase at intervals for the extraordinary period of forty-two years, towards the end of which time Germany was expected to pay annually £300,000,000, or half as much again every year as the total indemnity exacted from France after the war of 1870. Even that was not enough for a population which had been sedulously fed on lies by a class of politician who at times seem to possess among them no single sane and honest man. And an additional payment was demanded of a yearly sum equivalent to a duty of twelve per cent *ad valorem* on all German exports.

Opinion in Germany was sharply divided. All they had to pay with was an enormous deficit on the Budget, with the prospect of presently losing the Silesian coal-mines and having prohibitive duties placed by the Allies upon their exports. One party insisted that the Government should make no promise which it could not expect to perform; another, that what Germany wanted was peace, and that they had better sign anything required of them.

The first party, on the whole, carried the day. The German delegation in London made a counter-proposal based, very sensibly, on the idea of finding the present value of the forty-two-year annuities and raising that sum by means of a loan; but as they worked out the idea they favoured Germany on every detailed calculation to an extent which they must have known to be unacceptable. Apparently they expected a long and serious bargaining march. But, to most people's surprise, Mr. George leapt with alacrity at the prospect of a rupture. The proposal was rejected with every semblance of virtuous indignation. No time was allowed for the delegation to consult the German Government. A hurried second proposal, to pay the terms demanded for five years and then have the matter reconsidered, was tossed aside without consideration, and French and British troops proceeded to invade Germany, occupy more territory, and set up a new and artificial customs-barrier in the most unsuitable places, at which they proceeded themselves to collect the German customs.

The plan is very expensive, and utterly unprofitable. It involves a straining if not a breach of the treaty,[3] and it is likely, if any untoward event occurs, to provoke a war of the most humiliating and embittered kind—the war of a desperate and helpless population trying to rid themselves of foreign oppressors. But it has saved M. Briand's Government. If he had agreed to accept any German terms whatever, he would have been upset for not exacting more. But if he marches French and British troops into the heart of Germany no one can accuse him of lack of spirit. So for the present all is well; and as for the future, it is conceivable that the Germans will give way and make some impossible promise. That will increase M. Briand's prestige. It is more likely that they will simply sit still and let the Allied armies do their worst. Then there will be a chance of carrying out one of the darling aims of the French chauvinists, and annexing, or at least separating from Germany, all the German provinces which they occupy.

In face of these lunatic proceedings the German Government has behaved with considerable dignity and good sense, though naturally the German newspapers are running a little wild. It has announced its intention of appealing to the Assembly of the League of Nations, and although, not being a member, Germany cannot herself raise the subject, it may be taken as certain that some member will take it up on her behalf. This produces a most critical situation.

According to the Covenant, Article III, the Assembly may be summoned to meet "from time to time as occasion may require." But presumably it is the Council which decides whether occasion does require it or not, and no one can expect the Council to favour Germany's appeal. The appeal will only be considered when the Assembly has its next regular meeting in September. We shall then see whether the Assembly possesses the force and courage necessary to discuss freely and, if necessary, to condemn the actions of the two leading European Powers; or if the two can successfully silence all criticism. For my own part I think the discussion will take place; and that, for the first time since the war, the voice of an impartial third party wilt be heard in discussing the terms imposed on Germany by her conquerors. That does not mean the realization of the "enthronement of public right on the common law of nations," but it is one of the first steps toward it.

The League of Nations is in a position to say to France: "You are afraid of another attack by Germany; and to avert that danger you propose in various ways to follow a policy which will plunge Europe into continued distress. We hereby guarantee you against attack. Thirty-nine nations at present, who will shortly be increased to fifty-one, if not more, have signed a definite and unqualified contract to preserve your 'existing political independence and territorial integrity' against any 'external aggression'; and further, if you are attacked in such a way as not actually to threaten your territory or independence, all the States of the League will consider that an act of war has been committed against themselves, will apply the complete economic boycott to your enemy, and arrange plans for giving you immediate military support. We offer you here a far more effective guarantee of safety than you can possibly attain by your own diplomacy. But we demand in return that your foreign policy shall be frankly and sincerely a League of Nations policy; that you shall not make secret treaties, not set up inequitable tariffs, not plot the ruin of your late enemies or any other people; but work as a loyal member of the League with a view to the welfare of the whole."

The League says to Germany: "You complain of the undue severity of the treaty and the impossibility of carrying out its economic provisions. Commissions already exist, and you have taken part in them, for discussing these latter and fixing the terms of the reparation which you owe. But, beyond that, if there is any clause in the treaty which appears to any member of the League as 'threatening to disturb international peace or the good understanding between nations upon which peace depends,' it will, under Article XI, be brought before the League and considered. Further, if any clause in the treaty appears to 'have become inapplicable' or to give rise to 'international conditions which might endanger the peace of the world,' under Article XXIII the Assembly of the League may at any time 'advise their reconsideration.' You complain that the terms of the present treaty were imposed upon you, without discussion, by implacable enemies who had you at their mercy; that you have been made a sort of outlaw nation, without freedom, without colonies, without ships, sitting apart while the world is administered by your enemies. But at our Assembly table you will sit as an equal and free member, with the same rights as those who were lately your conquerors. We submit to you that this gives you a far better chance of improving your condition than another war could. Your lot must be for some time a hard one. That is inevitable, and we cannot think it unjust. You challenged the Entente to war, you staked all on victory, and you were beaten. Now you have to make reparation. But the recuperative power of a great nation is immense; and wherever you have been subjected to a definitely unjust or dangerous condition, we offer you a remedy. Wherever you may have a dispute with any other Power, we offer you a Court of Arbitration as impartially constituted as the wit of man could devise."

At present neither party quite believes this guarantee. If they did, it would probably be enough for them. It used to be said of Sir Edward Grey in the Balkan Conferences that he was not only sincere; he had the power of making other people see that he was sincere. If Europe is to be saved from new Great Wars, the Powers of the League must first of all be sincere in their undertakings, and next, they must convince the world in general of their sincerity. To that subject we must return later.

CHAPTER II
THE EAST

But the world is not merely threatened by the prospect of future wars. It is filled with wars at the present moment. There are quarrels and bickerings between most of the newly liberated states in eastern Europe; there is a war, sometimes avowed and sometimes underground, between Communist Russia and all her neighbours and rivals, a war whose tentacles reach far throughout Europe and Asia; and there are wars against the British and French in various parts of the East. Let us briefly touch upon a few sample cases.

I. Syria, Mesopotamia, Egypt, and India

The simplest case is Syria. In 1915, during the war, a Syrian National Committee, including representatives from Damascus and Mosul, negotiated with us through Sherif Husein, and we signed a document promising to "recognize and uphold Arab independence" in an area including the whole of Arabia, Palestine, Syria, and Mesopotamia, except (1) Aden and (2) the Syrian coast. Within the independent area we merely claimed for ourselves "a measure of administrative control" in Bagdad and Bosra—not in Mosul—and reserved any special interests of France. The French were informed of the negotiations immediately. They expressed themselves content with the possession of the Syrian coast, and agreed in our promises to Husein. On the strength of this agreement the Hejaz revolted, and Feisul's army, consisting mainly of Syrian and Mesopotamian soldiers who had formerly been in the Turkish service, fought as our allies to the end of the war. An attempted rising in Syria proper was crushed with great severity by the Turks.

In 1918 the Syrians welcomed the Entente armies as liberators, and were again promised their national independence, though this time it was to be under the guidance of one of the Entente Powers as mandatory. They asked that the mandatory should be England, but England had too much on her hands. The Syrians next asked for America; but America refused all mandates. France, meantime, had always claimed special rights in Syria, and England by a treaty made during the war had recognized Syria as a French interest. If they must be under France, the Syrian representatives specially demanded pledges that the government should be a civil government, that a certain degree of independence should be allowed to the natives, and that the country should not be occupied by French troops. How far these pledges were given and broken by the French; how far it was only we ourselves who gave assurances which we had neither the right nor the power to carry out, and thus unconsciously deceived Feisul, these are questions still in dispute. It seems unfortunately certain that the Syrians considered themselves betrayed. In the end, Syria was occupied by French troops; the native government was not recognized, but dispersed; there were raids and pitched battles, and the Emir Feisul, one of our most popular heroes during the Great War, was expelled from his throne and country. He is now an exile, and was for a time officially forbidden to land in England.

France so far has neither accepted nor asked for any mandate from the League of Nations, and appears not fully to realize the obligations undertaken by her in signing the Covenant of the League, or the pledge repeated in the Reply of the Allied Powers to Germany, "that the Mandatory Powers, in so far as they may be appointed trustees by the League of Nations, will derive no benefits from such trusteeship."

In Mesopotamia the British established themselves during the war after a long and chequered campaign by defeating the Turks and capturing Bagdad. The Indian soldiers and officials who were in command showed the most praiseworthy zeal and energy in proceeding at once to develop the country: to drain and irrigate, to plant crops, to establish order and good government in regions which had not known such things since a remote antiquity. The English were welcomed as liberators and made explicit promises to set up an independent Arab kingdom under a "measure of British administrative control." So much propagandist literature was poured forth on the glories of the independent Arab nation which the English were to create, that serious discontent was caused in Egypt. "Is a half-naked Arab to have independence, and am I not good enough to have even self-government?" wrote a highly educated Egyptian to a British official. Meantime the actual government of Mesopotamia became more and more severely effective, and remained entirely concentrated in the hands of the British. The expenses were enormous and the rate of taxation per head appears to have risen to four times what it had been under the Turks. The productivity of the country, however, was so great as to hold out a prospect of almost making up the loss, and the important oil-wells at Mosul were expected to do so completely. The native cultivators profited by the improved harvests and the increased area of cultivation, and the expenses of government were in part to be met out of the future oil profits. And the best British administrators were certainly beloved by their people.

The educated classes in Bagdad, the sheikhs and the ex-Turkish officials, became restive at the high taxation and the indefinite delay of "Arab independence." The turbulent desert tribes and the disorderly elements in general were disgusted at the good policing. But there was no general discontent, because personal assurances were given to leading Arabs that the Covenant of the League of Nations, which Great Britain had signed, laid down definitely that Mesopotamia was to be recognized provisionally as an independent nation and that the mandate was to be given to Great Britain. There would be, it was promised, a native Government with a British Resident to advise it, as in an Indian native state. Doubtless the Government would also ask for other help from England, especially in the matter of public works, irrigation, and the engineering of the oil-wells.

But the League issued no mandate. According to rumour, it had offered a scheme of mandate to the Great Powers concerned, and one at least of them had refused the terms. The precious oil, it was discovered, had already been divided by a private treaty between France and England, which left only a small fraction for the Mesopotamians and none for the rest of the world. There was no attempt to set up an Arab Government. Some beginnings were occasionally made of associating Arab officials with the Englishmen who did the real work of governing. But they were not wholehearted. A letter was accidentally divulged in which an English soldier said of the high Arab official attached to him, "I will soon make him lick my boots." There were symptoms of disaffection, non-payment of taxes, the resurgence of old discredited Turkish and German agents, open rebellions. And the Government replied by numerous executions and punitive expeditions. The bombing aeroplane, which had revealed itself as a very convenient weapon of war, proved an utterly disastrous instrument of police. The British liberators, who had come by the special desire of the population to establish a free Arab nation helped by friendly advice from British Residents, ended, according to Colonel Lawrence's estimate, in killing ten thousand Arabs and setting the whole country in a blaze of war. An army of over one hundred thousand men is now reconquering it. And at the same time, perhaps at the eleventh hour and perhaps too late altogether, that section in the British Government which believed in the League of Nations and wished scrupulously to carry out in victory the pledges it had given in time of distress, prevailed to bring about a definite change of policy. Sir Percy Cox and Mr. Philby were sent to Mesopotamia with instructions, so it was stated, to reverse the previous policy and try to set up that independent Arab Government which we had promised in 1915 and again in 1917, and ought to have set working before the end of 1919. The "rebellion" will doubtless be crushed, and the native Government may or not be successfully organized. There is a strong desire among the Arab leaders to have it based on a treaty of alliance with Great Britain after the Egyptian model, and not on Article XXII of the Covenant. In any case the task is infinitely more difficult than it was before so much blood was shed, and the original friendship of the Arabs turned to hatred. On simple men executive action makes a much deeper impression than policy. In Mesopotamia our policy itself was bad because it was not consistent. It was a muddle of two contradictory policies, resulting in confusion and hypocrisy. But the executive action seems to have been such as to make the chances of even the best policy very precarious. A government which multiplies the taxes by four and shoots and hangs its subjects in batches is seldom excused because of its good drainage or its progressive ideas.

The story in Egypt is shorter and perhaps less unhappy, but essentially similar. Early in the war, when Turkey joined the enemy, we declared a

British protectorate over Egypt, accompanied by a promise to give the country independence or free institutions at the end of the war. This in itself was a perfectly good and defensible policy, though, to be correct, it should have had the concurrence of Egypt. But in the course of the war Egypt became full of discontent. Experienced officials were wanted elsewhere, and inexperienced substitutes made mistakes. Labour in great quantities was required for the Army, and was obtained through native contractors or headmen, who practised the ordinary Oriental methods of extortion and corruption while professing to act by orders of the English. The peasant who was dragged off to forced labour, or compelled to buy his freedom by heavy bribes, blamed the British for both. At one time Egypt was garrisoned by large numbers of Australian troops, who had the habit of thinking of all Asiatics as "blackfellows," and whose ways of dealing with "blackfellows" were not of the gentlest. The seed was thus sown of a passionate hatred, partly just and partly unjust; and feeling was already ripe for explosion when it transpired at the end of the war that the British Government had no apparent intention of fulfilling their promise to confer on Egypt "free institutions." Open rebellion was impossible, owing to the presence of overpowering numbers of British troops; but a time of danger and infinite trouble, well controlled by Lord Allenby, led at last to the appointment of a Commission under Lord Milner, which grasped its almost desperate problem with great courage and skill.

Among other curious misfortunes, it turned out that the word "protectorate" had been translated into Arabic by a term which denoted the sort of protection that is extended to an outcast or a person with no national rights. The Commissioners were met on their arrival by a universal boycott, and by constant threats of assassination. They lived in considerable danger, and no Egyptian would be seen speaking to them. But tact and patience gradually broke down the boycott; and a much larger measure of agreement was obtained with Zaghlul and the moderate Nationalists than had at the outset seemed possible. After inquiry, the Commission has taken the line of recommending, first, the cancellation of the Capitulations, or special privileges granted to European states, which have paralyzed the progress of Egypt for several generations; the separation from Egypt of the Canal zone, as a special British interest and of vital importance to the Empire; the retention of British advisers in two posts, the ministries of Justice and of Finance—a safeguard without which the European Powers would not consent to forgo the special protection of the Capitulations; and in other respects the establishment of Egypt as an independent national state. As far as is possible to forecast, it looks as if this settlement would succeed.

The history of recent events in India is too large and complicated a subject to be dealt with here. But in its main outline it has been curiously similar to that of the other regions of the East. A wonderful response from almost the whole continent to the need of Great Britain during the war; blunders of the War Office and reactions of discontent; German propaganda; Turkish and Pan-Islamic intrigue; repressive Press Acts and Conspiracy Acts; passive resistance, dangerous riots, and widespread conspiracies; the severe and sometimes lawless coercion of the Punjab; the savage massacre of Amritsar, and at last, amid great obstructions and hesitations, the passing of the Montagu-Chelmsford Act and the conferring of a new and liberal constitution upon India. It is the same story as in Egypt and Mesopotamia. So much time was wasted in doing the wrong thing, that when at last resort was had to the right thing the right time was past. The Indian Government was faced with great difficulties and very real dangers. Its errors have been so signal and notorious that public opinion is apt to forget or ignore the admirable skill and patience with which most officials steered their districts through periods of extreme strain. But reforms long promised were delayed until too late. The executive plunged into excesses which will not be forgotten for centuries. And when the long-hoped-for reforms at last have come, it may be that they come to a people too exasperated to give them a fair trial.

II. An Eastern Policy

The policies here described have been so full of errors that it is hard to derive from them a very clear moral. Government without principle has many conveniences; if life consisted of isolated moments it might be entirely successful. But life is continuous, and human beings have memories and expectations. And almost any policy that is continuous and consistent and true to itself is more likely to succeed in the end than a mixture of momentary expedients and plunges for safety. It is conceivable that a perfectly resolute and unfaltering military coercion of India, Egypt, and Mesopotamia might have succeeded. But such a policy, if it was ever possible, is certainly so no longer; and also it would hardly be a policy for avoiding international strife. And that is the subject we are considering.

If we look below the mistakes of policy and administration committed by the British or French Governments, we find underneath the surface a profound and instinctive resentment of the Moslem East against the Western Powers. The Western Powers, which for convenience we term Christian, have been for some centuries far more efficient than any Moslem state. The West has increasingly taken charge of the East; beaten it, managed it, "run" it, governed it, and in some cases exploited it. Western government, or at least British government, has been just, incorruptible, impartial, strong, intelligent, far beyond ordinary Eastern standards. It may have been unsympathetic and grossly expensive; it may, in spite of the unexampled personal integrity of the whole governing class, have led to the presence in Eastern countries of undesirable money-seekers. But it has been, on the whole, essentially and undeniably good, efficient government, backed by a military power which committed few excesses, lived on its own pay, and never failed in an emergency. No one who studies even superficially the history of average Oriental governments, from Morocco or Bokhara to Oudh, can be surprised or sorry that they have been superseded by the better governments of the West. The peoples of the East themselves have gained by Western penetration; nay, more, they are conscious of their need of the West. But they have had too much of it; they resent it, and they are frightened of it. The Moslem nations have lost their independence one after another. At the beginning of the Great War only one Moslem Power remained free and powerful—the Turkish Empire. At the end of the war there was not one.

The Turks were not popular in the East. The Syrians and Arabs hated them almost as much as their Christian subjects did. The Turkish peasants of Anatolia suffered cruelly under the exactions of Constantinople, especially in the matter of military service. But all through the Moslem East ran the consciousness that the Sultan, with all his faults, was their own man. He was the acknowledged Head of the great majority of Moslems in the world. He was, above all, the last barrier that seemed to protect them from the overwhelming flood of Western aggression, and the last great Moslem figure which enabled them to preserve their self-respect.

While the Turkish Empire stood, the Moslem peoples, though fallen on evil days, could think of Islam as an independent and even an imperial entity. In places, doubtless, they had to kiss the feet of dogs; but their Caliph still ruled masses of Christian subject populations and still was master of the capital city of the world. With the fall of Turkey, the last free Moslem state was gone. Not here and there, but everywhere throughout the whole world, the faithful were set beneath the heel of these rich, drunken, pork-eating idolaters with their indecent women, their three Gods, and their terrific material civilization. "Pan-Islamism," as Mr. Toynbee says, "is only an extreme example of the feeling at the back of almost any modern Oriental movement we may examine. It may take aggressive forms, but the essence of it is a defensive impulse. Its appeal is to fear, and if the fear of the West could be lifted from off the minds of the Oriental peoples, its mainspring would be gone."

The problem of our Eastern policy is to remove that fear. And that ought not to be so very difficult. The essential fact to grasp is that the East needs us far more than we need the East. We need markets; but that idea is only suggested to us by the fact that Eastern peoples want our goods. We do almost everything better than they do. They want our textiles, our knives and tools, our engines and ploughs, our books, our learning. They cannot make railways or ships without us. They cannot work their mines or oil-wells except by Western help. They cannot really govern their countries satisfactorily without European advisers. The language of Article XXII of the League of Nations Covenant is quite correct when it says that "Certain communities formerly belonging to the Turkish Empire have reached a stage of development where their existence as independent nations can be provisionally recognized, subject to the rendering of administrative advice and assistance by a mandatory until such time as they are able to stand alone." At present "they are not yet able to stand by themselves under the strenuous conditions of the modern world."

They ought to want us, and if left alone they would want us. We have frightened them into fighting and hating us by forcing ourselves upon them instead of waiting to be asked. We have conferred incalculable benefits on India: the benefit of protection from invasion, of comparative protection from plague and famine, of social order, of administrative justice, to say nothing of roads and railways, and the enlivening force of Western knowledge. We have immensely increased the prosperity of Egypt, we have put down all kinds of Oriental abuses and protected the fellaheen against *corvées* and extortions and tortures. We were in process of beginning to perform the same services for Mesopotamia. But in the latter regions at any rate—for in India our roots are far deeper and the problem is more complex—the people did not want us. We only held them and did them good by force. And the chief reason why they did not want us was fear. We came to them with machine guns and bombing planes as conquerors and masters, having destroyed the only free Moslem Power; and they found it difficult to believe in our good intentions. We came to them, most unfortunately, also with specious promises which we made in time of need and broke in the days of victory.

The right policy is something very easy to state and extremely difficult to carry out, even for a single-minded and clear-headed Government. It needs first, perhaps, an effort of imaginative understanding more far-reaching than has ever yet in history been demanded of an Imperial Power. Only those who understand the East can win the respect and confidence of the East. But in the meantime, if we cannot fully understand, there is a way at least to make ourselves understood. Justice is the passport to confidence all the world over. And our first business is to act quite simply and sincerely up to all our engagements. We undertook certain obligations when we signed Article XXII of the Covenant. We should make the "wishes of these communities a principal consideration" in deciding whether we should go to them at all. We should really treat them "as independent nations," and should honestly give them "administrative advice and assistance until they shall be able to stand alone." And we should not allow our minds to be confused by thoughts of gain, nor our advice to take the form of horse, foot, and artillery. Two illustrations may make this point clear. An experienced and very successful administrator was asked a few weeks ago whether he would accept the post of adviser to a certain Moslem Government. He said, "Yes, upon one condition. That there is no British army anywhere in the country." That is the right and wise spirit. The second is even simpler. One of the most obvious and matter-of-course obligations laid upon imperial administrators and civil servants is that they shall not embark in trade or in any way make a profit out of the administration of their office. That is the right rule. The Empire should set an example of the behaviour that it expects from its best servants.

When we apportioned to ourselves the German colonies, we specially declined to take over their public debts. And when protest was raised against this proceeding, we stated definitely in our official Reply: "It would be unjust to make this responsibility rest on the Mandatory Powers, which, in so far as they may be appointed trustees by the League of Nations, will derive no benefit from such trusteeship." Is it entirely quixotic and idealist to hope that, even in post-war conditions, a great nation may remain true to her word?

It seems at least as if the only alternative was to hold these Eastern territories by armed force, and that is no longer possible. It might be possible to hold by force India alone, or Egypt alone, or Mesopotamia alone. It is not possible so to hold all three. We must govern by consent of the governed or not all.

CHAPTER III
RUSSIA AND ITS BORDERS

Another group of wars and threats of war has its centre in Moscow. All the States on the borders of Russia—Finland, Lithuania, Poland, the Ukraine, Hungary, Rumania, the new republics of Georgia, Armenia, and Azerbaijan, and the kingdom of Persia—are either at war or in fear of war or just recovering from war with Russia, or from civil war fomented by Russian agents and propagandists. Inside Russia itself, civil war has never ceased since the first outbreak of the Revolution in 1917. It is true that the civil war has been largely helped by foreign munitions and stirred up by foreign intrigues. But that only shows that—as the world is now organized—there is something in the present Russian Government which makes foreigners as well as Russians wish to take up arms against it. It may have been—I think strongly that it was—exceedingly unwise for the foreign Governments to intervene in the domestic troubles of Russia, but no one can pretend that the civil war was entirely created by foreigners. The rebellions were there before the foreigners joined in, and it is even thought by good judges that the opposition to the Bolsheviks might by this time have been successful if it had not been damned in Russian eyes by its foreign alliances.

For us the question is how the Russian Revolution has become such a plenteous and intense cause of strife. It is, of course, impossible to pass judgment on the whole of a vast movement with the very inadequate information that is now accessible to an average Englishman about Russia. Even the French Revolution, which has been studied by thousands of observers and historians, is not yet judged. The sum of infamies and high achievements is too complicated to add up. And the Russian Revolution is probably even harder to value than the French.

I. THE CIVIL WAR

It would be a mistake to forget the elements of simple early-Christian brotherhood which seem to characterize the Russian peasant. It was well known before the war how the members of a workmen's *artel*, or trade community, when trade was bad, would divide their earnings equally and all starve, if need be, together, without any attempt by the luckier workmen to save themselves at the expense of the others. The glowing descriptions of Mr. Stephen Graham cannot be entirely without any basis in fact. And the people of Tolstoy and Dostoievsky have evidently a most rare capacity for sainthood and martyrdom, as well as for aberration of mind. Present-day Russia has been described by an eminent Socialist as "a nation of artists governed by brutes," and the phrase is probably true of the old Russia also, and the Russia of centuries back. Communism comes easily in Russia, and so does submission to tyranny.

It must also be remembered that the Great War, among its many aspects, involved the most frightful and bewildering oppression of the poor and weak. As was said quite truly: "Millions of poor men in divers regions of the world have been dragged suddenly and without any previous action of their own into a quarrel which they neither made nor desired nor understood, and in the course of that quarrel have been subjected again and again to the very extremity of possible human suffering." The war naturally and inevitably created in Europe a passionate wish for some revolutionary transformation of a world in which rich and clever people in parliaments and governments had the power of inflicting such pains upon the poor. The peculiarity of the Bolshevik movement was, as one of its rare English admirers puts it, not so much that it wanted a particular kind of Socialism or Communism, but that it wanted it *now*. The world has seen many revolutions and many Socialist governments; but they have never really established that paradise of the poor which was advertised in their prospectuses and doubtless nursed in their hopes. Most failed altogether. And those which succeeded went wrong. They coöperated with "bourgeois Liberals." They extended the franchise, they improved the condition of the working classes, they established well-to-do workmen and peasants with a stake in the country and a conservative bias; but they never really did what was wanted. They always stopped short. They developed the middle-class virtues. They left still in existence a capitalist class which preached the merits of thrift and hard work and was interested in trade; and of course they left always somewhere an oppressed class. The under dog was still under.

The Bolshevik remedy was very direct and simple. It was to disarm everybody who had any share in prosperity, and distribute firearms to those who had nothing else. Only when he was armed and the rest of the people unarmed could the real proletarian—the man who had no savings, no talent, no education, no notable good qualities, nothing that makes for success in life—hope to beat the men who always outstripped him. It is strange that even in a moment of extreme misery such a theory could have established itself in any country as a principle of government. But the military collapse of Russia gave it a unique chance. The common soldiers, anxious to fight no more, already possessed arms. They had merely to murder their officers and the thing was done. The rest of the population was unarmed and helpless. And meantime the peasants, though almost untouched by revolutionary ideas, were amenable to one particular bribe. The revolutionaries offered all the peasants of Russia their masters' land without any payment. They could simply take the land, and kill or not kill the owner as they pleased. There was no punishment for such killing. According to strict Communist principles, the land was not to remain in the peasants' possession. It was to be the property of the State. But this principle had to be dropped in order to induce the peasants to coöperate with the revolutionary town workmen. Whatever may be said in favour of this revolution, there can at least be no surprise at what Lenin calls "the frantic resistance" of the upper and middle classes of Russia. The policy of the Government was announced on January 23, 1919: "The present is the period of destruction and crushing of the capitalist system of the whole world. . . . In order to establish the dictatorship of the proletariate it is necessary to disarm the bourgeoisie and its agents and to arm the proletariate." It is to be dictatorship in the strict sense: the power of a man with a gun to do what he likes with those who have no guns. There is to be no democracy or representation of the dispossessed classes. If they were represented they might recover power. Only those known to be faithful to the new Government are to vote. All persons of property must be dispossessed, from landlords to small shop-keepers. Rich peasants must go; even "middle peasants" at one time had to go; only the poorest peasants and the poorest town workmen should rule, assisted, of course, by those educated people who would accept the new régime and establish by deeds beyond doubt their hatred of the bourgeoisie.

The control of a country by a small minority is always difficult. It needs methods of "terror." But this minority had first to acquire the control and then to maintain it. Its task was more difficult and its methods had to be more violent than those of its predecessors. The "terror" of the old Czarist Government or of the French Revolution must be superseded by the more drastic method of what was called "mass terror." The secret police, whose activities had made hideous the record of the Czarist Government, and who had fled for their lives at the first outbreak of the Lvof and Kerensky Revolution, returned from their lurking-places to put themselves at the disposal of the Bolsheviks. This legion of devils had something to sell which the new Government badly needed. On the analogy of the *Comité de Salut Public* there was established the All-Russian Extraordinary Commission for stamping out all trace of resistance to the new order. Spies were placed everywhere (Proclamation, October 17, 1918). No distinction was to be made between Czarist reactionaries and unorthodox Socialists, such as the Mensheviks and Social Revolutionaries (*Russkaya Zhizn*, May 10, 1919). Enormous numbers of "hostages" were arrested. At any sign of conspiracy outside, large numbers of these were shot. The assassination of the Bolshevik Uritzky was repaid by the execution of five hundred citizens. Yet, just as in the most furious days of the French Revolution, the terrorists were always complaining that there was not enough terror. "The continual discovery of conspiracies in our rear . . . the insignificant extent of serious repressions and mass shootings of White Guards and bourgeoisie on the part of the Soviets, show that notwithstanding frequent pronouncements urging mass terror against the Social Revolutionaries, White Guards, and bourgeoisie, no real terror exists" (Official Weekly of the All-Russian Extraordinary Commission, No. 1, Moscow, September 21, 1918).

Trotzky in comforting language explained that the object of the mass terror was not really the extermination of all non-communists, or all Russians who did not attain the full standard of poverty and orthodoxy. "The proletariate says: 'I shall break your will because my will is stronger than yours, and I shall force you to serve me.' . . . Terror as the demonstration of the will and strength of the working class is historically justified" (Trotzky in *Izvestia*, January 10, 1919). Eventually, of course, when all Russia was submissive and all Europe Communist, there would be a gentler régime, and the proletariate would show their true beauty of character. And it would be a mistake to ignore the real reforms which seem to have been carried through in certain social services, notably in the care of children, the attempt to develop popular education and the putting down of drink. But in the meantime terror was reënforced by ingenious petty persecutions and indignities, reënforced by starvation. Those who joined the Red Army had three times the ration of food allowed to several categories of the civil population. No one can wonder that suicide—that last irrefutable evidence of unbearable oppression—became extraordinarily common, especially among the educated classes,[4] and that "frantic resistance" broke out where it had any prospect of success.

II. Russia's Neighbours

But what of the war outside Russia? Why could not the Russians be allowed to conduct their revolution and settle their form of government by themselves? It would be very desirable if they could. And doubtless it is the aim to be striven for. But the trouble is that Bolshevism is to its adherents a revelation and a new gospel, and they have the same zeal for converting the rest of the world as had the French Revolutionaries or the followers of Mohammed. "The program of the Communist Party is not merely a program of liberating the proletariate of one country; it is the program of liberating the proletariate of the world" (authorized pamphlet by N. Bukharin, July 24, 1918). This is to be achieved by "a bloody torturing and heroic fight." The methods are to include every known form of intrigue, corruption, forgery, and the like, and the plan is to be the same in all countries. Revolutionary workmen are to be armed, including common soldiers, tramps, prisoners, and all the utterly dispossessed of the earth, except, of course, those who have Conservative, Liberal, or Labour Party views; and then are to work their proletarian will on the rest of the community. The "national will" is to be disregarded: "The interests of Socialism stand far above the interest of the right of nations to self-determination" (Trotzky, *Izvestia*, March 8, 1918). "All our hopes for the definitive triumph of Socialism are based on this conviction and on this scientific prevision, i.e. that a revolution like the Russian can be produced in all the nations of Europe" (*ib.*). In the Treaty of Brest-Litovsk the Bolsheviks were compelled to sign a clause promising not to conduct "any agitation against the State and military institutions of Germany." "But both the Russian Government as a whole and its accredited representative in Berlin never concealed the fact that they were not observing this article, and did not intend to do so" (Joffe, *Izvestia*, January 1, 1919).

The belief that by some single violent change in social, political, or economic conditions human life as a whole can be suddenly transfigured is one that clings to many minds, and by no means the stupidest minds, of the present age, in spite of much disillusioning experience. It does seem to them at moments as if only some one thing was wrong with the world, and as if that one flaw must surely be definite and remediable: some one bold step is all that is needed—say, the abolition of the family, or of property, or of competition, or of wages, or of interest, or of compulsory law, or some other of the fundamental institutions of society.

To our ancestors it was the abolition of heresy. To the Turks, the abolition of all Christians in Turkey. To such people at such times the normal method of trying to correct the worst abuses by persuading the majority that they ought to be corrected, and of seeking individually to live a better life and to help one's neighbours, seems tedious and ineffective, if not hypocritical. But one thing that is clear is that revolution means "frantic resistance," and the stronger the faith and energy behind the revolution the more deep-reaching is the resistance likely to be.

Russia's neighbours see what seems to them the infinite misery and impoverishment and retardation inflicted by Bolshevism; and they are naturally indignant and alarmed at the secret propaganda of Bolshevism within their own borders. In normal times perhaps they need not have been afraid. But since the war every state is unstable; every state has a large discontented class. The small republics in the Caucasus, barely able to support themselves in freedom, are maddened to find their constitution threatened by Russian bribes, their malcontents and bad characters armed with Russian rifles and machine guns, and their public men assassinated. Georgia and Armenia are probably doomed. Hungary and Finland have gone Bolshevik and returned, each process being accompanied by hideous persecutions and murders, the reprisals being naturally the worst. Germany, in spite of all treaties, has been exposed to constant propaganda and has had one or two bad outbreaks of violence. Poland has been and still is— whether through her own bad policy or otherwise—on the brink of compulsory Bolshevism. Human nature being what it is, and human politics a little worse than private human nature, it is inevitable that Russia's neighbours should be constantly afraid of her and intensely anxious to see her again under some more normal government; some government which, whatever its political bias, would leave its neighbours to govern themselves and accept the ordinary conventions of civilized society.

Nay, one can even understand anti-Russian policies that seem at first sight intolerably aggressive. The Poles, among other demands, are anxious for the independence of White Russia, the region north of the Pripet, of which Minsk is the chief town. They wish it either annexed to Poland or else made independent, but at any rate cut off from Russia. The claim seems monstrous. But it has its excuse. The White Russian peasantry are said to be peculiarly ignorant and devoid of national feeling; the land-owners and well-to-do classes are mostly Poles. Is it surprising that the Poles of Poland hate the idea of handing their countrymen over to a Russia which will, as a matter of course, set the peasants to burn their houses, destroy their cattle, and hunt them themselves down like vermin? And when that is done, they reflect, Bolshevism will only be nearer to Warsaw.

Like the early Moslems, the true Bolsheviks care more for their faith than for territory. In dealing with Lithuania, which is at present a comparatively quiet little peasant republic, the Russians offered her a large slice of territory beyond what she was entitled to or wanted. Why? Because it was a thoroughly Bolshevized area, and might be expected to spread the faith—or the poison—into all Lithuania. A nation, or a government, in that state of mind cannot be surprised if its neighbours regard it with anxiety.

It is a curious fact that revolutionists so often regard themselves as pacifists. Many were even conscientious objectors during the war, and there is no reason to doubt that they were sincere. But they do seem to be confused thinkers. To hate your neighbours, whom you know, and love your neighbours' enemies, whom you do not know, is a consistent and not uncommon frame of mind; though the element of love in it seems less important and prominent than the hate. But to expect European peace and good-will by means of a revolution in all countries argues a lack of understanding not far removed from madness. Every revolutionary outburst since the war has been marked by ferocious cruelties and followed by still more ferocious reprisals. Revolution leads not to peace, but to reciprocal reigns of terror, first Red and then White, till the exhaustion of suffering produces some sort of equilibrium.

The war, among its many evil lessons, has inculcated the gospel of impatience and of force. "When you want a thing, take it from some one, and if he resists, knock him down." It is the doctrine which destroys human societies as it destroys the peace in men's own hearts. If we want peace, we must simply unlearn that creed and go back to the old Liberal doctrine that is at the root of sound politics everywhere: "If you think something is right, try to persuade your fellow citizens of it; try your hardest, but remember that you may be wrong, and until you succeed, have patience."

CHAPTER IV
PRE-WAR AND POST-WAR CAUSES OF STRIFE

The war has left behind it a great number of small wars or guerrillas. Most of them have their explanation in some ordinary excess of nationalism or revenge or greed. The Serbs, intoxicated with their new greatness, are still causing war in Albania and Montenegro. The Rumanians recently invaded Hungary, in spite of all the thunders of the Peace Conference, because they had been robbed by Austria-Hungary and wanted revenge and reparation. The Hungarians have alarmed all their neighbours and forced them into a defensive alliance, which now calls itself the "Little Entente." The Lithuanians and Poles have fought, but been reconciled by the mediation of the League of Nations. The Armenians have been massacred again, under the eyes of the French army of occupation in Cilicia, where they had gathered under a repeated guarantee of safety given by France and England. The Turkish Nationalists are holding out very unsuccessfully in the centre of Anatolia against a Greek army carrying out the directions of the Supreme Council. The Turkish peasants are increasingly reluctant to take arms again. The Koreans have helplessly declared their right to independence from Japan, and are apparently being reduced by a terrible persecution.

These are the mere belated effervescence of the passions of the Great War. The hate and pride which are the basis of nationalism and which were so violently stimulated by the events of the war cannot be expected to die out at once. It was calculated a short time ago that there were twenty-seven "wars" of one sort or another in progress. But they will presumably simmer down as social conditions become more normal.

It is interesting to observe that two of the greatest causes of war, according to the judgment of normal times, are now not actively operating. Before 1914, if one was asked to name the main causes of war, the answer would have been, first, competitive armaments, and, second, protective tariffs and the competition for markets. These causes will remain fully as dangerous for the future, but it so happens that none of the existing wars is directly due to either.

I. Armaments

In one sense, indeed, armaments are actually operating now as a cause of war. There are far too many firearms lying about. America, England, and France have made very lavish gifts or sales of lethal weapons to various bodies with whom they sympathized. And the arms have by no means always stayed in the place for which they were intended. Guns which we sent to Denikin were sold by corrupt officials to the Bolsheviks, and passed on by them to the Afghans to use against us on the Indian frontier. Such things cause some deaths and some laughter, but are not permanent evils.

No European nation, except those actually compelled, has made much progress towards disarmament. It is said that Great Britain has actually made the greatest reduction, but both in numbers of men and in expenditure our standard is fantastically higher than what was forced upon us by German competition in 1914. It is impossible to reduce our forces in a really drastic way as long as our commitments are so large and—perhaps we must add—our policy so inconsistent and provocative. Peace with Russia, a settlement with Mesopotamia and Egypt on the lines laid down by the Covenant and the Milner Report, the evacuation of Ireland, the execution of the Montagu-Chelmsford reforms in India, and the extension of similar reforms to Burmah and the much-suffering Ceylon, will permit us really to envisage for the first time a satisfactory measure of disarmament. The air force is already greatly reduced. The vast size of the navy appears to be utterly unjustified, at any rate by conditions in Europe. The French army is far beyond the economic powers of France to support. The same seems to be true of Italy, and is certainly true of Serbia, which is still calling conscripts to the colours. Greece is vastly overarmed; but Greek policy, though erring on the ambitious side, has probably been more sagaciously guided under M. Venizelos than any in Europe. The fall of that great man, due mainly to the prolonged economic distresses of Greece, will probably cause a resurgence of Mustapha Kemal and the Turkish nationalists. Meantime the Russian conscript army, though apparently ill-armed and ill-supplied, is overwhelming in numbers and is led by officers of the old régime, experienced and not absolutely incompetent. The Russian army is far the greatest and, in a political sense, the most dangerous, in the world.

But it is not the actual armaments, ruinous as they are, that are the essential poison to civilized society. It is the competition in armaments. That has now been abolished throughout Europe. Slowly, unequally, reluctantly, the armaments which, in Lord Grey's words, went uphill under the lead of

Germany, are now, under the same lead, groping their way downhill. There is only one great nation which, if words are to be believed, thinks seriously of starting a competition in armaments. It has been announced, more than once, by the American Government that, like Germany in the years before 1914, they have arranged a naval programme which will effectually put an end to the British command of the seas and give the United States "world primacy" (see speech of Mr. Daniels, Secretary of the Navy, in the *Times* of September 1, 1920). Since the British Empire is a scattered series of communities dependent for their communications upon the sea, and in particular since the population of Great Britain is absolutely dependent for its food on the free use of sea transport, it has been generally acknowledged in Europe that the sea-power of Great Britain was necessary to its existence. British sea-power has never been challenged except by definite enemies in pursuit of a definite war policy. If the United States were seriously to embark on the same policy as the late German Government, it seems as if all other causes of war must sink into insignificance beside this gigantic and deliberate one. But, in spite of some bewildering symptoms, it can hardly be believed that this conclusion is possible, at any rate until America has definitely and finally refused to be a member of the League of Nations.

Relations between Great Britain and America have of late been dangerously strained, partly owing to causes outside our Government's control, but in part owing to the scandal caused in America by certain developments of the Peace Treaty, and by the excesses of the Government forces in Ireland. A wise policy may help to heal this growing breach, and if America accepts in some form or other membership of the League of Nations, it ought to be possible in friendly discussion to arrive at some understanding on the question of naval armaments.

The problem of armaments is put in the very forefront of the Covenant of the League, immediately after the constitution of the League itself. By Article VIII—

The members of the League recognize that the maintenance of peace requires the reduction of national armaments to the lowest point consistent with (*a*) national safety and (*b*) the enforcement by common action of national obligations.

The Council, taking account of the geographical situation and circumstances of each State, shall formulate plans for such reduction for the consideration and action of the several Governments.

Such plans shall be subject to reconsideration and revision at least every ten years.

After these plans shall have been adopted by the several Governments the limits of armament therein fixed shall not be exceeded without the concurrence of the Council.

The article goes on to recognize that private munition factories are objectionable, and must somehow be dealt with, and to lay down that all members must interchange "full and frank information" about their armaments and programmes. And the next article constitutes a permanent Commission to advise the Council on the execution of the provisions of Article VIII and other similar matters.

The cautious language of the Covenant on this subject is due to the inherent difficulty of the subject itself. It would be absurd to lay down that every member of the League must disband its forces forthwith; the League could hardly undertake to go to war in order to compel some strong Power to disarm. And it is obvious that different nations need different degrees of armament. The chief difficulty is that disarmament ought in justice and prudence to be simultaneous all round. It is only by the compulsion of a lost war that Germany has been compelled to disarm while her enemies stand round her with large armies, and even in Germany the process is evidently very difficult to enforce. Too many rifles and machine guns have got loose in private hands. No League could compel Poland or Rumania to disarm while the Red Army of Russia stood waiting across the frontier; or compel Great Britain to disarm while the northwest frontier of India is constantly attacked, while the Bolsheviks are in Persia and British officials are besieged in Mesopotamia. This difficulty will remain even when the world begins to settle down and the countries of Europe are no longer governed by their War Offices. On the other hand, economic pressure, as well as Liberal feeling, will make for the reduction of armies and navies. It may be difficult to get volunteers for military service, and it will certainly be dangerous to impress conscripts. There will be a stronger and more genuine popular demand for disarmament than for most of the desirable provisions of the League Covenant, and Governments dependent on the popular will may find their hands forced. But in the main disarmament must depend on the restoration of confidence; though probably it is true in most cases that if the disarmament comes first the confidence will follow.

II. Markets and Food

The second of these great causes of war, protection and the competition for markets, has somewhat changed its aspect since the comparative exhaustion of the world supplies of food and raw material. Before the war, nations chiefly wanted to sell. Markets were the great object of ambition, and tariff walls the great means of offence. Great Britain, of course, kept her doors everywhere open to the trade of the world. It is one of the decisive marks to her credit in the apportionment of the comparative guilt of the nations in preparing that international atmosphere which made the war of 1914 possible. But if she had chosen at any moment to close her doors, she could have injured grievously every other great nation throughout the globe; and the British Tariff Reform Campaign was one of the excuses used by the German Government to frighten their people into a war spirit. When Austria wished to ruin Serbia she simply put a prohibitive duty on the import of pigs.

Now, since the war, what most nations want is not in the first place markets; it is food and raw materials. They have not, of course, abolished their tariffs, but their first anxiety is to be able to buy food. Austria does not want to keep out Serbian pigs. She begs for them, and Serbia will not let her have them. The most consistently and narrowly protectionist nations, like France or Australia, no longer concentrate on forbidding their neighbours to sell to them. On the contrary, they refuse to sell food and raw material to their neighbours. The policy of keeping the food and raw materials of the British Empire for British consumption is already widely advocated and has powerful champions in the Government. As long as it is confined to palm kernels, this policy, though bad from almost every point of view, is not fatal. But if ever it were to be carried consistently through, it would mean war. The British Empire holds such a vast extent of the earth's surface that it has inevitably given hostages to fortune. So huge an empire can only be tolerated if it behaves tolerably. If we keep to ourselves and use for our own profit all the overwhelmingly large stores of food and raw material which by our vast annexations of territory we now control, thereby reducing other nations first to a stagnation of trade and then to starvation, the natural and inevitable answer to such a proceeding would seem to be a world crusade for our destruction.

This is the chief point, apparently, in which the influence of what is called "capitalism" seems to be a direct cause of war. Great capitalists, or those impersonal organizations of capital which seem likely now to supersede the individual capitalist, are normally strong influences for peace. They need peace for the success of their undertakings and are in danger of ruin if war breaks out. But they do at times stand to gain enormous sums by concessions and monopolies and by control over materials which are the subject of an intense demand from great masses of people. And no doubt one way in which they will seek to get these monopolies and controls is by putting pressure on Governments for so-called patriotic reasons to exclude foreign competition. This is a very real danger.

The Covenant of the League of Nations has not dared to insist on free trade. Obviously it could not, since the majority of the member nations are against free trade. But it does lay down certain rules to check aggressive protection.

All the territories transferred by the war from the possession of Germany and Turkey to their conquerors are subjected to the principle of mandate. They are not held as possessions. They are held "as a sacred trust for civilization" with the express purpose of securing the "well-being and development" of the native populations. In particular, the mandatories agree to guarantee "equal opportunities for the trade and commerce of other members of the League." As the membership of the League is increased, this will practically ensure the "open door" to all nations in the mandated areas. It seems also clearly to forbid the establishment of national monopolies. If a mandatory finds copper-mines or oil-wells in its territory, it is bound to develop them as "a trust for civilization." Any profit it receives must be in the nature of wages for work done. A mandatory may not exclude or hamper the trade of another member of the League by tariffs,[5] much less keep the oil for the exclusive use of itself and its friends, as is at present proposed by England and France in Mesopotamia. The condemnation of this proposal by the Assembly of the League in November, 1920, backed by a vigorous protest from the United States, has, it may be hoped, made such a violation of the Covenant impossible.

In territories not mandated as a result of the war, but otherwise similar to the mandated areas, such as the pre-war colonies of the various Powers, these rules, of course, do not hold. Yet it may be hoped that at least they will be recognized as good rules, to which approximation should be made as circumstances permit.

In all their dealings, moreover, members of the League agree (Article XXIII) to "secure and maintain freedom of communications and of transit, and equitable treatment for the commerce of all members of the League." The language of this article is a little vague. One can trace in it the influence of a struggle. But at least it forbids tariff wars, and it gives the League a handle for interference in case of any very great iniquity. It does not forbid national monopolies; but a monopoly in foodstuffs which came near to inflicting famine on other members of the League would, under it, at least give cause for remark. And no clause, however strong, could in practice be sure of attaining more. The League has to be built out of nations as they already exist, and the rules of the League out of their public opinion. The real danger here, as in so many other cases, lies not in the caution and moderation of the language used in the Covenant, but first in the questionable sincerity of the nations in carrying out the pledges signed by their representatives, and secondly in the possibility that, through ill-will, or fear, or self-interest, or mob-passion, or some other disastrous influence, the ex-enemy Powers be not quickly included in the League. Not until all Central Europe is in the League can the world begin to breathe freely.

CHAPTER V
THE LEAGUE OF NATIONS

We have considered many parts of the world and many aspects of the present world settlement to see what seeds of future war may now be germinating and what means we have of making them harmless. And in every case we are brought back to the one great creative idea which this war has produced, the League of Nations. The earlier notions of the League, as issued, for example, about the year 1909 by certain American bodies, centred upon the development of compulsory mediation or arbitration and the setting up of a recognized permanent Court of International Law. The flaw in this conception, operating alone, is a certain rigidity and barrenness. It left states to work separately until they quarrelled or saw a quarrel approaching, and only then, when the atmosphere was already bad, it expected them to meet and accept arbitration. A great addition to this was Sir Edward Grey's conception, already put in practice during the Balkan Wars, of an extended *entente cordiale* embracing all Europe and America. In his time France and England, England and America, England and Italy, had formed a habit of cordiality and frank dealing. When any trouble arose, the ambassadors had the habit of meeting freely and discussing the trouble with perfect frankness, almost as members of the same Ministry might do. This tendency was helped by the enormous increase in international conferences, commissions, and bureaux. And during the Balkan crisis of 1912-13 it was in process of being extended to include Germany. Thus there was the habit of frequent coöperation and mutual confidence. Unfortunately, this friendly spirit depended on all parties being generally content with the present condition of affairs; Germany was not content, and so the *entente* idea was balked. Under the League the nations are already forming a habit of consultation and coöperation on non-controversial matters which should be of immense help in dealing with differences when they arise. Another great formative idea was contributed by General Smuts, the principle of the mandate. He foresaw that there would be at the end of the war an immense appropriation of tropical colonies; he knew that the rivalry of the Great Powers for the possession of such colonies was one of the chief sources of international strife; and he saw that the right outlet was to put an end to the treatment of colonies as "possessions" or mere sources of wealth to the colonizing Power. The populations that are not able to stand alone should be taken in trust by the whole League of Nations, which should appoint a particular Power in each particular case to carry out the trust. Again, the great stirring of discontent among the labouring classes in almost all parts of the world led to the formation of a special International Commission on

Labour, which has so far met with great success. It will in general have the effect of raising the conditions of the most backward peoples to something like the level of the best.

And lastly, when all these things were in train, the policy for which both Great Britain and the late Czar of Russia had striven so long and vainly would at last become feasible, and the nations might consent to disarm.

Thus the Covenant of the League, an unpretentious but well-considered document, the result of repeated criticism and study by many of the best minds in Europe and America, attempts to meet and check all the visible and predictable causes of war.

There should be no wars of ambition. They are to be met by absolute coercion. The League can make it certain that deliberate war undertaken for national aggrandizement will end, not in profit, but in ruinous loss.

There should be no wars caused by the irresistible desire to escape from foreign oppression or intolerable conditions. They are made unnecessary by provisions enabling any oppressed nation to lay its case before the Assembly or Council and obtain such redress as the most disinterested tribunal can give.

A war which is caused by the emergence of some clash of interest or unforeseen dispute between two states cannot, in the nature of things, be made absolutely impossible. The League opposes to that danger, not a blank wall, but, as it were, a series of springs calculated to exhaust its force; a court for points of law, mediation for points of policy, compulsory delay and reconsideration for all disputes whatsoever. It will be a strange dispute which, given honest intentions on both sides, lasts through all the checks provided by Articles XII to XVII and plunges nations into war at the end of them.

Wars caused by rivalry for the possession of colonies and rebellions caused in colonies by unjust exploitation are, as far as regards mandated areas, provided against by Article XXII; for the other colonial territories, which do not come under a mandate, at least the way of safety is shown.

Wars caused, or made more likely, by the mutual prejudices of nations, by their habit of working always apart and in secrecy, are met by the immense field of international coöperation which the League proposes, and its absolute insistence upon frank interchange of information.

Wars caused by exclusive tariffs or national monopolies of material are in part provided against by Articles XXII and XXIII and in part by XI.

Wars which might be caused by domestic revolutions, as in Russia, are made less likely by the Labour Commission, which assures a remedy for any labour conditions in a particular country which are so bad as to incur the active condemnation of the world.

But it is impossible by mere enumeration to be sure of meeting all the causes from which some new war may start. The League, in the last resort, falls back on the mutual trust and good-will of its members, and particularly of its members' representatives, secured partly by the common interest in peace and partly by the habit of coöperation for ordinary affairs. The *esprit de corps* of the League's permanent Secretariat, with a professional interest in the preservation of peace and good-will, is a new and important factor in the world's life. Any member of the League has the right to bring to the attention of the Assembly or Council "any circumstance whatever affecting international relations which threatens to disturb international peace or the good understanding between nations upon which peace depends."

In America the Covenant of the League is apt to be represented as a terribly drastic and tyrannical document. Cartoons show John Bull, or some equally repulsive abstraction, dressed in khaki, dragging away American youths to fight enemies of the League in remote parts of Asia or Africa. But on this side of the Atlantic it is generally criticized for not being drastic enough. It does not make war formally impossible. It does not bind all its members to make war on any Covenant-breaker. It does not even bind any member of the League to accept the decision of the majority. It leaves its members almost as free as if they were outside. They are pledged to accept, if they ask for it, a decision of the International Court; they are pledged to the principle of mandate; they are pledged to boycott any deliberate war-maker. But that is practically all. The League's true weapon is not force, but publicity.

The truth is, and it is a truth of fundamental importance in political matters, that no structure can be more rigid than the material of which it is made. Engagements between human beings must needs be as elastic as human nature itself. Had the Covenant laid down that every member of the League was to make war or peace, or change its foreign policy, in obedience to the majority of the Council or Assembly and in disregard of the wishes of its own parliament, the result would have been either that no nations would join such a League or that, if they did, the League would break at the first strain.

The principles laid down in the Covenant are, in the judgment of the present writer, principles long recognized and absolutely right. If generally acted on, they will prevent war. If generally neglected and broken, they will allow wars to ensue. This fact seems to be pretty generally recognized among the more reputable statesmen of Europe. But it remains unfortunately true that they are principles implying a considerably higher standard of international morality than has hitherto been consistently observed by any nations, even the best. If absolute fidelity to the Covenant by all its signatories were necessary for the peace of the world, the world would have a very poor prospect before it. What we must aim at is as much fidelity as possible. There are great difficulties. America is absent. Germany and Russia are absent. France cannot yet quite escape from her war psychology. But if Great Britain is faithful, it will be hard for other nations to be obviously and grossly false. The European neutrals, like Switzerland, Holland, and Norway, will be clear voices for justice and fair dealing. The beaten nations, when once admitted, will probably be on the same side, since when wrong-doing begins it is the weak who are first to suffer. And, after all, all human beings have a strong dislike of injustice, when they do not directly gain by it. The great majority of the fifty-one members of the League will be disinterested on most questions of dispute, and will therefore form a good tribunal of opinion.

But the mere clash of contrary selfishnesses produces no sound equilibrium. The League will not succeed unless in some of the great nations, above all in Great Britain, there are at the head of affairs statesmen who believe firmly in the principles of the League and are capable both of effort and of self-sacrifice for the sake of them, and behind the statesmen a strong and intelligent determination in the mass of the people to see that the League is made genuinely the leading force in international politics.

The present disorder of the world is one of those in which the remedy is not obscure, but perfectly ascertained. The only difficulty lies in applying it. The nations of the world must coöperate; and for that they must trust one another; and for that the only way is for each Government separately to be worthy of trust.

It will be long, no doubt, before this end is consummated or even approached. The foregoing pages have shown how far from perfect is the practice of even the most stable and advanced nations. And the tendencies set up by the war, with its infinite reactions and ramifications, are almost all such as to make vastly more difficult in each case the necessary effort towards good faith and good-will. Yet, if the difficulties are greater, the necessity is greater also; and after all the war has brought its inspirations as well as its corruptions. The craving for this Peace which has not come is, I believe, still the unspoken and often unconscious motive of millions who seem, at first glance, to be only brawling for revenges or revolutions; it lies, like a mysterious torment, at the heart of this storm-tossed and embittered world, crying for it knows not what.

FOOTNOTES

[1] The other points were briefly: Evacuation of Russia: restoration of Belgium; of France; transference of Alsace-Lorraine; territorial settlement of Italy; autonomy of peoples of Austria-Hungary; settlement of Balkan States; of Turkey; restoration of Poland; and lastly a League of Nations—though President Wilson never used that somewhat inaccurate phrase. I should like to acknowledge here my indebtedness to the admirable and convenient series of publications issued by the American Association for International Conciliation, 407 West 117th Street, New York.

[2] See Keynes, pp. 60-102. A provision was kept enabling all such private property to be confiscated in case the German Government should "voluntarily fail" to fulfil its engagements. But this also was dropped by the British Government in October, 1920.

[3] The Allies are apparently acting under Part VIII, clause 18, of the treaty. This gives them the right to "take such other measures as the respective Governments may determine to be necessary" in case of "voluntary default" by Germany in the payment of her dues under Part VIII (Reparations). A failure by Germany to disarm sufficiently gives the Allies no right to increase the area of their occupation, since the present occupation is specifically laid down in the treaty negotiations as the means of enforcing disarmament. Nor has Germany yet actually committed a voluntary default in the payment of her reparations, since the first payment, £100,000,000, is not to be completed until May 1, 1921. I am informed on high authority that the Allied case probably rests on the point that they judge by their debtor's manner and by statements which she has made that she intends not to pay by May 1; according to English law this would apparently give them some right of taking immediate action.

[4] The remnants of the more distinguished "intellectuals" are now gathered into two or three "salvage houses" and looked after by Maxim Gorky. [He has now fled.]

[5] Except in Mandates C (Pacific Islands, etc.), where Australia successfully refused to submit to any economic restrictions. See, however, the definite pledge given by the Allied Reply, p. 78, above.

Milton Keynes UK
Ingram Content Group UK Ltd.
UKHW040816051024
449151UK00004B/261